MW00881616

TESTED
NEVER
DEFEATED

a memoir by
Bryant Reed

~ 𝖲R ~ Sea Ross Publishing

Tested Never Defeated

First Edition

Copyright © 2018 Ben Longoria and Sea Ross Publishing

All rights reserved.

Cover art by Velina Martinov

E.L. Francis, Editor

Ben Longoria, Chief Editor

Published by Sea Ross Publishing

Printed by CreateSpace, An Amazon.com Company

ISBN 9781724924964

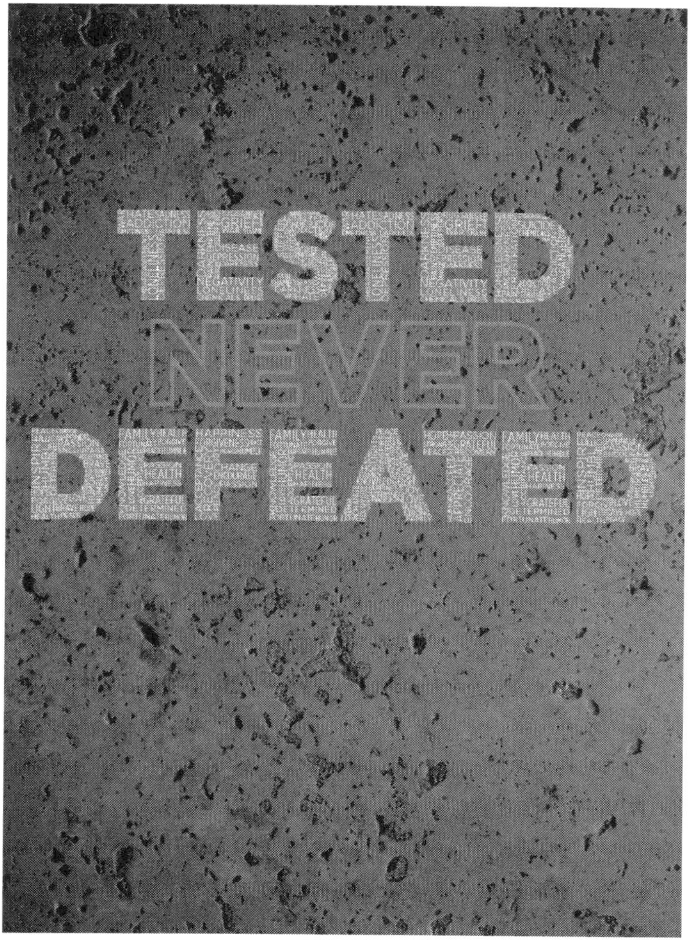
TESTED
NEVER
DEFEATED

PREFACE

The standard dictionary definition of success is *the accomplishment of an aim or purpose of the desired outcome*. When writing this book, I considered if someone would want to read about someone who hadn't attained specific traits that society labeled successful. My bank account doesn't harbor numbers with a plethora of commas. I haven't made an appearance on TV or been sought for anything grand. I'm not recognizable like a celebrity you follow or value for their fame and fortune. Books from people with those accomplishments tend to fly off the shelf and become best sellers. People see a glamorous lifestyle and want to obtain it. When you see me, my exterior doesn't seem extraordinary and certainly doesn't warrant massive amounts of attention. When I speak, however, you feel my energy and start to see who I really am.

It is only in the definition of the word success that I found clarity in what I was doing. Making it in this world, to me, is about more than money and status. I don't sugar coat the price I paid to get to the level I'm at now. I'm always striving to increase my spiritual, physical and mental wealth. That is my only aim. My words carry weight, even if they come from outside your normal scope of influence. They come with a message that needs to be heard, absorbed and applied. When you open your mind to these ideas you can increase your willpower, success will follow, in whatever capacity that is to you.

CHAPTERS

ACKNOWLEDGEMENTS

I remember listening to an influential sermon that discussed the importance of every individual you meet. The speaker explained that those who treat you badly and people who show you love both have an influence over the trajectory of your life. He said to choose wisely how to react to both types and that would lead to a successful and balanced life. I wholeheartedly agree.

I feel that power in the strength of my parents more than anything. Through the good, bad and ugly of growing up, they paved the way for me to use this platform to tell my story. In writing this book, I will discuss some demons that I dealt with and some major hurdles I encountered before building the life I have today. I want to be extremely clear, there is no correlation between suffering in silence and how much my parents loved me. The lessons they taught me and the moments we shared all ended with a positive outcome. I don't remember every Christmas, birthday or vacation as a child. I hardly remember the states I lived in, nor do I have an in-depth understanding of the lineage of my family. I do remember the power of our family dynamic. No matter what we went through, we were family through and through.

To my mother, Tressy Mason. I cannot begin to express my appreciation for the extent to which you tried to shield me from the world. When you were dealing with your own health issues, you never let that affect how we grew up. I never saw you in pain, though as an adult I now know how much you were. Circumstances in life were not always perfect, but you made sure my brother and I were always first and no one ever surpassed us as the number one in your life. Even when you remarried, it would have been easy to shift focus, but you still put us first. Even though we didn't always agree, I thank you for the many lessons of inner strength and respect you bestowed upon me. You are the reason I made something of myself, the reason my path never strayed too far from the straight and narrow. The love I have for you is unconditional and forever. I will always be your baby.

To my father, Carvie Mason. I remember watching you and your work ethic every day. Not just some days, but every day, making sure we needed for nothing as kids. You sometimes worked two jobs and showed us what a stable loving father should be. I feel you made it your priority to teach us how to respect and love my mother. You treat her as your queen so that when I married, I knew how to pay it forward. I know you didn't always have the energy to be at every event I had, but through every accomplishment you were always in my corner. You are a rock, and without even knowing it, you showed me how to get through so many situations in my life. I hear you in every decision I make. For that, I say thank you, for all the tough-love moments and teaching me through your character and actions, rather than just your words.

To my loving wife, Kimberly Turner. I was in a very dark place before we found each other again. You brought me back to being the person I always knew I could be, the person I always wanted to be. I am glad we parted ways earlier in our relationship, per your advice, so that we could grow as individuals and learn how to be better equipped for this stage in our lives together. I honestly think if I ended up anywhere but North Carolina, I would have spent the rest of my life comparing everyone and everything to the love I've always held and always will hold for you. The journey here was worth every mile because it means I can be the man you spend the rest of your days loving. Thank you for letting me be myself and for listening, even when I am making zero sense. You feel my frantic passion, you understand my work ethic and not once have you made me compromise the person I am for you. I love you and what we are, and everything we continue to become on this journey of life.

To my brother, Andrew Reed. I looked up to you, though I never showed it. I've always been a little too ego driven to fully realize how much you impacted my decision to make something of myself. You set a standard that, even to this day, I reflect on as a pillar to reach. The stories of you standing up and physically fighting for me showed your true dedication and love for me. Though life during college and deployments drifted us apart, I believe we share a bond bigger than a phone call or a holiday spent together. Without your example, I would be stuck in the small town we grew up in, doing nothing, and becoming nothing. I owe a great deal of my success and drive to you. Thank you, big brother, I find so much comfort in the rekindling of our relationship. Even though I am much bigger than you, I will always be your little brother.

To my son, Jaden. I love you with all of my heart. I know one day you will have the chance to read this book and reach out to me about our time together. Just know that despite any mistakes I made, or the distance apart, not a day goes by that I don't think about you. We had so many great times and through pictures, I reflect back to the times we shared. I'm not the person you may grow to think that I am, and hopefully this book will help you see the truth. I encourage you to not take everyone's words to heart, but to instead find your own answers There is so much love for you on the East Coast, I hope it reaches to where you are. No matter what, daddy always loves you, and you will always be with me.

To my beautiful little girl, Scarlett Grace. The day I first laid eyes on you I knew that I couldn't love anything else more than you. That was it, you had my heart. I will spend the rest of my life making sure you are protected from any and everything. The universe has given me another chance at being the father I know I can be, and I won't let you down. Life can be tough, and I hope when you are of age to read this book that you appreciate the man that is your father. I don't ask you to mirror my footsteps or be anything greater than what you desire to be. I just ask that you always put me, your mother but most of all your dreams and aspirations first. I will be here for you through all the hiccups in life. I love you!

To the Turners. From day one you welcomed me into your house with no judgment and only the expectation that I treat your daughter right. Through my deployments, you sent care packages and always kept me updated on the status of your daughter, whether we were dating or not. You have listened, understood, and supported me and what I do. My appreciation for our holidays spent together, and the simple dinner you guys occasionally whip up, goes a long way. As you say every time I'm there, "Turners are family first," and I too am family, you've always treated me as such. Each of you brings joy to my life and I thank you for opening your minds and building a relationship without judging first. Thank you.

To anyone that has inspired me or pushed me in the direction of greatness, know that I am truly blessed to have had your help. My thanks to family, friends, and clients as well! I'm proud of the time I spent with amazing people pursuing astounding things. I also owe a huge thank you to those who told me I wouldn't amount to anything, and people that constantly tell me, "you can't," when I profess my goals. Your negativity and jealousy (unknown to you) towards me, turned into a fuel that I wake up every day and burn. You are the chip on my shoulder. Yours are some of the most motivating words I hear anytime I want to give up. Thank you, and please keep putting your limitations on me so I can prove you wrong!

It's time to see what made me into the person I am today. I sincerely hope everyone enjoys this journey as much as I enjoyed writing it. This is not my last book but, personally, it's probably the most important. Enjoy.

INTRODUCTION

This will not go down as a standard autobiography or motivational self-absorbed book. You know, the ones which claim to give a blueprint for success that's not practical for the typical person. The type of book that makes huge claims about having the ability to drastically change your life in seven days, make you millions of dollars or lead you to believe a life without negative thoughts is actually possible. You can find those type of books in abundance, yet they all seem to fall short of delivering what they promise. I am not promising anything if you decide to take this journey with me. Nope, nothing at all.

What this is for me, and hopefully for you, is a reflection of my life, my failures, accomplishments and how they shaped the person I am today. The trials, downfalls, the moments of severe depression, sprinkled with satire and just enough down-to-earth storytelling that anybody will be able to relate to. This is for those of us grinding day in and out at work, raising a family and slowly navigating through this challenging life. Those of us that face challenging roads daily, yet somehow chose to confront them head-on and persevere. Maybe you are struggling with your own demons and something in my story helps to shake them loose. I don't think there are enough books written by people in the trenches of life, this is that book. I've dealt with negative circumstances for a great portion of my life and I spend each moment ensuring that I don't slip back into darkness.

I have to be honest, everything that I remember is crystal clear, but there are so many things that I simply don't remember. While most people can recite the name of their first-grade boyfriend or girlfriend or even a family trip they took while young, my mind has somehow blocked out a huge percentage of the usual stories people discuss when speaking about their past. I've learned to live with the fact that I'll never remember huge blocks of elementary school or childhood friends. I don't know what year I was here, there, who I knew, or what we experienced during our brief or extended encounters. I have accepted that I may never fully know who I was then. Let me reiterate, the stories in this book are one hundred percent true and more than just fleeting memories in a mind I consider to have underachieved. These stories have defined my mindset as I have navigated to this point in my life. I fully integrate them with the practices I preach as a business owner, health and wellness coach, father and husband.

I'm not looking for sympathy or for anyone to fix what I can proudly say isn't broken. Some of my family may not even understand my need to publish this book. It certainly might be difficult to understand something you didn't experience personally. I am in no way attempting to embarrass my family, nor am I casting them out as bad people. If you read my acknowledgments you will know just how important they are to me. I also don't want to cast myself as someone bigger or better than anyone. I'm sure you have a wonderful story as well, it probably hasn't been all green grass in your life either.

Some of the words in this book will be harsh as I try to invoke enough emotion to illicit and insight to the events responsible for creating the person I am. Some things may be offensive or seem embellished. This is simply my account of how things took place. There's a lot I hid from the world in an attempt to toughen up and fit in rather than communicate and receive the help I needed. The burden rests solely on my shoulders, and you should know I am okay now, and proud of the person I have become. I needed every lump life dealt me, and without them, my path, my story, may not exist.

I'll do my best not to bore you with unnecessary

details or words just to fill blank space. Understand, part of the reason I am writing this is for self-therapy. Having a huge audience would be great, but if one person reads what I write and is motivated to better themselves or know that you are tested in life, but never defeated, me leaving it all out there is well worth it.

There will be a moment for all of us when our minds leave us and our bodies will cease to steal oxygen from this world that will ultimately forget us. To leave something behind for someone else to become a better person is what I feel the creator has in mind for each of us. Showing people that they don't have to be scared to tell their story is another goal of mine. This book is where I set out to leave part of my legacy to the world. Though I am still writing my story daily, I'm glad I realized that putting it on paper now would be the best way to preserve what I still remember.

I've chaptered this book into specific events in my

life that are worth telling. Some stories come with life lessons, and some of them I tell just to free my mind. They've been locked inside my head and writing them has become somewhat of an amnesty for the mental prison I held them in for so long. As a kid, I spent a lot of time writing as well. Some of the things I wrote during that time make an appearance between chapters. You will get to read exactly what I was feeling during those moments. I didn't realize what I was writing during those times would hold any weight to anything I did today, but it helped me with laying out my story. I hope it helps you understand me a little better. Looking back, writing has always been therapy for me.

I've never gone into the amount of detail I'm giving each topic in my entire life, verbally, or written. Laugh with me, hell, laugh at me, cry with me but most of all realize that we each have our own story. This is mine.

JUNE 1ˢᵀ, 2005

We all grow up with dreams and hopes of becoming someone better, someone who has the power to affect certain aspects of the routine we are imprisoned in. So, who am I to believe that my being should be even slightly different? My aspirations were plotted out in my brain at the beginning of my existence, hard-wired in my DNA. It's hard to see past the blurry and difficult circumstances I struggle with every day. I relate to a bipolar state and it makes me think that I am the problem. Maybe I am the one that needs fixing for the way I've handled things that have been thrown my way. When I stop and think, it puts ideas like this to rest.

Human beings can become better than the hardships they are dealt in life. After all, for every negative you endure, someone is going through something ten times worse. That tells me I have no right to complain. It shows me that my life isn't hell but maybe a momentary pause, or halt, in the development of the character I will soon become. That doesn't mean I can't voluntarily share my story and through professional channels allow it to be cycled through the minds of my peers. This just means I have to allow myself the realization that, together, maybe we can bring about a change in the world that has been unheard of during my generation. And to contribute to such a movement, I must continue prepping my mind for one of the most powerful inspirational life I can lead.

To some, words to paper are just that, static symbols, boring, flat, and without meaning. I can't describe the sensation of discovering the beauty in assembling simple letters together to create something so complex it makes others pause and think, maybe even cry. Thinking allows an opportunity to understand the truth. Through discovering what is real, we will finally be able to knock stereotypes and negative ordeals that hold us back and keep us from seeing one another as the unique individuals we are, breaking the division that keep keep us from loving and feeling as human beings.

I come to tell you that I am nothing special. I'm just a small-town boy who speaks to those that understand better through words on a page rather than spoken language. I am just a boy with a story, overcoming struggles of my own, and I intend to change lives with my words, spoken or written.

A QUICK FAST-FORWARD

THROUGH CHILDHOOD

I don't remember most of my childhood and unfortunately, specific dates and years of age I did certain things escape my memory. Most of my memories come from my teenage years, my parents divorced when I was young. Since then, the man who I consider to be my real father raised me with my mother. They instilled discipline from the very beginning using the kind of old-school tactics that don't fly in today's softer society but served a purpose back then. It was the kind of discipline where you better be sure the crime you committed was worth the time because they were ready to drop the hammer.

I felt I was always a bright kid and reading and

writing were something that I did very often. In fact, there were moments I remembered wanting to be a professional writer when I grew up. I wrote short stories and poems in my free time during many boring moments in my life but was always too shy to share them with the world. I dominated grades up until late middle school when I started to rebel against everything. I don't know what clicked, but at some point, I put on my screw-the-world armor and wore it all the way to the military.

Puberty came with a new sense of being bigger than my britches, which often got me into deep trouble. Most people experience, something I refer to as a highlight reel, for their wrong-doings, punishments and achievements as children. The things, that while going through them seem like the end of the world or the greatest accomplishments, but are now things to laugh and reflect upon during family get-togethers.

I remember being grounded for an entire

summer. I think that might have been the year I lied
about my report card. It was the end of the year. We
received our report cards and mine, of course, was
not good. I knew my parents would ground me for a
week or worse if I brought those kinds of grades
home. It was summer break when a kid's whole
purpose was to have fun. I didn't want to ruin mine
but there would be no fun with grades like that. I
decided it would be a better option if I just lied about
receiving my report card.

I told them it would arrive in the mail in a few
weeks for them to sign and mail back. I even had the
audacity to tell them I'd done extremely well that
semester, making A-B honor roll at the very least. The
truth was D's and C's with an A in gym class. I never
understood how a kid could fail gym class! I spent
most of my high school years signing up for every
gym class you could take, but I digress.

I thought they would forget all about that measly
little piece of paper. A few weeks rolled around and

they asked me about my report again. Little did I know they had already spoken to my teachers and knew the truth. My parents always seemed to have the upper hand when I decided to try my hand at besting the parenting system. That was when they served up the crippling punishment of being grounded for the whole summer with only the freedom to read books. I heard my brother laughing during family movies, going outside to play, while I was in my room reading and writing. I don't think it ended up being the whole summer, but it was a big enough chunk that I still remember today.

I read my butt off that summer to show them the punishment couldn't affect me. I have always been the type that if you try to inflict your will onto me I'll push back and turn the table on you. If you want something to bother me, I'll go out of my way to show you it doesn't affect me in the slightest. It is not healthy, but I am damn good at bottling emotions.

All their punishments seemed to serve a purpose.

I rarely repeated an offense. All I had to do was tell the truth, something they fully expected every time I was in a pickle, but something that was also very hard to do. I hated being told what to do then, and I still struggle with it to this day. I learned my lesson. Instead of lying about those bad grades, I should have just been honest and let the chips fall where they may, even if it wasn't in my favor.

Another shot from my highlight reel of life is the time I went full-stupid at the swimming pool. I can't recall my age at the time, but I remember almost drowning due to my impulsive behavior. I had spent the day playing in the pool with my brother while visiting my biological father. There was no supervision and I felt like my brother, who was three years older than me, was more than enough to keep me safe. I couldn't swim at the time so I hung out in the really shallow end.

At some point, I got out of the water and was relaxing on a poolside chair when these unusually

large wasps started flying around me. I hate wasps,
even in adulthood, they seem to be my kryptonite. As
the wasps flew aggressively over my head, I made a
hasty decision and jumped right into the deep end of
the pool. What transpired next was a whole lot of
panic and someone frantically trying to get me out of
the pool. I came out spitting water, scolded for such a
mindless action. I didn't care. I was more concerned
about not being stung. I would have much rather
drowned than faced the aggression of a wasp. People
still find it funny how at the lengths I go to avoid those
flying kamikaze insects, as if their sting comes with a
death sentence.

Although I lived in several other states while
growing up, the small town of Franklinton, North
Carolina, is where I called my home in my teenage
years. I remember hating it there, I always felt like I
didn't fit in. I spoke differently than most of my peers
and they made sure to let me know it all the time. By
different, I mean proper, a thing I consider normal yet

I still get teased for it today. I just don't like slang, and I consider it lazy.

It didn't help that my dad had a thing for making me dress like a picture out of the 1970's like I was from his era or something. It's another memory I find humorous now, but I remember a specific outfit that scarred me every time I had to wear it to school. An orange turtleneck tucked into a pair of tan corduroy pants. This was all coordinated with black loafers and a thick black belt around my waist.

My dad was constantly working on his barber skills and always hooked me up a high and tight with a part somewhere on the side. If I wasn't wearing turtlenecks or Bill Cosby sweaters (long before everything went downhill for Cosby), I was wearing fluorescent diamond patterned windbreakers. I didn't mind those so much, but the colors were always too bold for my taste. This was during the sports jersey and t-shirt era, the Timberland boot and rap music era, the fresh fade from the barber shop era. With

25

those outfits, I stood out in a bad way.

Sports were the one thing that kept me grounded and at least semi-cool. I was a great athlete and earned the honor of all-conference in some sports, above average in others. I was even featured in the local newspaper a few times. Without sports, I probably wouldn't have associated with most kids my age. I always got a sense that no one really liked me. Girls, what girls?

I went through a stage of pretty massive front teeth, I spoke like an adult, and I never really hung out with the cool kids. It's funny, although it should have been the opposite, girls liked me more when I was disrespecting teachers, dressing like a thug and getting bad grades. Socially awkward, is how most would describe me during those times. Even around family, I was extremely reserved, hell, I still am today. My philosophy has always been if you don't have anything profound to say why waste words? I hate small talk.

I went through so many phases as a kid. There was a time I thought I was going to be a rapper, B Dot Reed Dot was my rap name. I still have some of the raps I wrote but I am way too embarrassed to share them with anyone. When 50 Cent first came out, I listened to his lyrics and obsessed over his music videos, trying to mirror his every move. I wore a du-rag in a ponytail and made gun noises while watching his videos. I imagined I was the one that had been shot nine times and made myself bulletproof. It must have been something about relating to his pain and the tenacity of his story. In my head we were friends despite the reality he didn't even know I existed.

There was a time when I was straight gothic. I wore black and listened to dark music, most of which my parents confiscated when they read the labels or heard the lyrics. Again, there was something about the pain and the anti-establishment in the words that I connected to. I went through a prep phase where if it wasn't Lacoste, Polo, or a tight American Eagle brand, I wasn't going to wear it. I didn't even like the look of the clothes, but I pursued whatever identity I felt would get me the most attention.

I spent so much time trying to find out who I was and trying to fit in and still was never able to pinpoint the qualities I needed to be to be considered one of the cool kids. I think the phases I went through, are the reason that I can relate to so many different types of people today. If you listen to a wide array of musical genres, broaden your fashion choices, and possess the ability to alter your persona at any moment, you can blend into most environments, with an emphasis on blend. The cost of being a social jack-of-all-trades was being unable to be true to myself. Blending in, without a clue who you really are, is exhausting and unfulfilling.

Soon after I started attending Franklinton Middle School, in mere days, the bullying began. Kids then, much like today, have a natural talent to sniff out weakness, especially in kids who lack a strong sense of identity. Unfortunately I was that vulnerable kid. I was shy and quiet, traits some people misconstrued as a sense of superiority. They thought I believed I was better than them. Not true at all.

After class one day, while the teacher was gone, I went back to retrieve a textbook I accidentally left under my seat. Up until this moment, the school bullying never crossed the line into actual physical confrontation, but that day was different. Three kids and myself reenacted a scene straight out of the WWE. Professional wrestling was big at the time, and everyone was trying new moves on their friends without executing them fully so no one would get hurt. I was new so it appeared no one applied the same caution to my well-being. In fact, during most of the bullying I experienced the people observing, the others kids, found my situation humorous. Those three kids came into the classroom, surrounded me, punched me in my stomach and grabbed me to mimic one of the worst wrestling moves you can do, the pedigree. The move involved chicken-winging my arms to the side and locking my head between one of their legs. I didn't bother resisting because I honestly didn't believe they'd actually follow through. I thought they were just messing around, you know, kids being kids.

As I was held tightly in place, my captor jumped into the air and dropped me. My head crashed onto the cement floor. I was knocked out cold. I woke up in the room alone with a painfully large knot on my forehead. With tears streaming down my face I went to the principal's office to let him know what had been done to me. It was in vain. The principal didn't care about some wrestling stunt, after all we were boys, so he shrugged it off as run-of-the-mill horseplay and foolishness.

My parents came and picked me up from school that day because I was too dazed and in too great of pain to continue. They asked why I didn't at least stand up for myself. I had no answer to that question.

30

After that event a switch went off inside my head. That was the first and last day of my life that anyone got physical with me. No longer would I cower from aggression towards me. I'd stand my ground from that point onward to the present. Funny enough, my social life took a turn for the better once I made that change.

Eventually I grew into my own. My looks improved and my parents relaxed some of their dress standards. They started to give me the freedom to pick out my clothes. I always kept the outfits simple. I was most comfortable then, as I am nowadays, wearing shorts and a t-shirt. This period took place late in high school. I had some decent friends by then, who I'd keep in touch with long afterward.

My situation improved and in my junior year I was nominated for homecoming court, along with four other kids in my grade. This was a shock to me because I still didn't feel very popular. I made the finals and got to walk out on the football field with a chance of becoming homecoming prince. As fate would have it, I would go on to lose to the same kid that pedigreed me when I was younger.

What person isn't struck by nostalgia when they reminisce on aromas of a childhood kitchen? My mom always ensured that my brother and I were well fed. Some of the best meals of my life came after some of the longest days. I can still hear the chicken crackling in oil on the stove and the bread machine whipping up a loaf we'd eventually top with icing and devour in a sitting. My mother, sweating, would run around the kitchen frantically as she poured her heart and soul into each and every morsel of food she prepared for us. It's one of the ways she shows her love for her family. I've never stopped appreciating the value of a home cooked meal because of her. I call her from time to time to get a recipe, or to brag about a meal I cooked for my wife. We used to joke that every time my mother fired up the stove, she put her foot into the pot, an expression only a true Southerner would understand. Her mind was always on her two little boys, and me being the baby, she made sure no one mistreated me.

The best meals usually went hand in hand with grueling days laboring in the yard. The essence of hard work is something my parents instilled in me from the beginning of my early teenage years. If there was outside work to do, I was right there in thick of it, bringing to life my dad's vision of how our yard should look. There were many times, going into a project, I couldn't see his vision. Yet, it somehow always worked out for the best once we were finished. Whether it was moving logs to the burn pile, push mowing the four acres of land we owned (in the dead of summer), or planting bushes in a newly landscaped area, I was expected to get my hands dirty and never complain.

I won't lie and pretend that I enjoyed any of this work. I didn't know it then, at the time, but my parents were preparing me for the future. I would tell them that when I was an adult I'd move out that I'd live in an apartment, free from any of the hassles of sweating outdoors. Never again would I rake a leaf or cut a blade of grass. I'd pay someone to do it for me or it wouldn't get done. Unfortunately, as a homeowner now, that youthful boast turned out to be a huge mistake.

I think the best thing my parents did was not allow me to take the easy way out during my summer breaks from school. Most kids were going to summer camp or prepping for an activity-filled hiatus from learning, but in my home it became character building time. A few summers they sent me up to Virginia to spend a month or more with my grandparents. I think with the stress I put my parents through during the school year, those weeks were a much-needed break for them. Having become a parent myself, I appreciate having a break from the kids from time to time.

Although I absolutely loved spending time with

my grandparents, and the abundance of food in the house, life there was no vacation. My grandpa owned a construction business. I had to accomplish any task he needed help completing. Most days consisted of early mornings before the sun came up, a quick breakfast that my grandma prepared, and hopping in his old Ford truck en route to a job site. During those summers, I helped him hang drywall, scale tile ceilings in a school, build a deck on a house, and, the worst job of them all, scrape and replace kitchen floor tiles. It was sweat equity at its core. Any time I felt like slacking or tried to complete a task my own way- which was almost always taking a shortcut- he always reminded me that there was a specific way to do things. There was no deviation allowed. My grandpa was tough, and I love him for that.

My only reprieve came on days when my body's natural alarm clock would go off. Laying there in bed, I'd listen for the familiar sound of his footsteps stumbling around getting dressed, but was instead met with the sound of him snoring. It was rare and he did this without telling me his intentions the night before. Relieved, I'd fluff my pillow back up, close my eyes, and rest my tired body. I truly felt like an adult in those moments, worked to the bone yet content that I was accomplishing something.

By the time the summer ended, I knew what it felt like to have a full-time job! Before heading back home he would hand me a check for all the hours of work I had completed. Working with my grandpa was the first time I saw hard work go hand in hand with not only building grit but monetary value as well. I was tremendously grateful as it allowed me to buy the clothes I wanted to wear to school. A new pair of shoes and new threads meant that I could step into school a little more confident. Those summers were extremely important to constructing my discipline, drive, and perseverance.

I truly believe in the notion that we become the

example your parents set for you, sowing the seeds they plant throughout your life. In my eyes my dad is the king of hard work. He's the kind of guy that could be dead tired and still drive us to and from visiting family whenever. There were points when he'd work multiple jobs, often in a single day, in order to provide for us. By day he would grind out a long IBM shift and by night he would load freight onto UPS trucks in the dead cold. He always stepped up to any unforeseen obstacle. Among his greatest challenges was raising two boys who, at first, resented him. As we matured we eventually grew to accept and appreciate him for his sacrifices and being a great father. I get goosebumps thinking about the tenacity he showed every day, attacking life without complaint. His example imprinted itself onto me and shaped my work ethic.

I've always felt I stood out in this regard. It's as if I were wired differently than most others. I can endure copious amounts of pain, both physically and mentally. Where most people search for relief or look for human comfort and reassurance, I thrive in my own mind, enduring whatever life throws at me.

While playing football one year, I suffered a broken wrist. It was my fault. I put my hand up to stop a running back coming full speed, an instinctive reaction that had severe consequences. He kept running and I, of course, went down. I felt a crack and the referees stopped the game as I laid there holding my wrist. There were no tears, though I was in a significant amount of pain. The coach came out on the field and asked me if I was okay, a silly question in my eyes because he could clearly see my limp hand. I told him I was good but that I thought I broke my wrist. I couldn't move it, and I felt tremendous pressure. Coach told me to stay calm, another ridiculous thing to say since I was already as cool as I could possibly be under those circumstances.

The medical staff took me to the hospital where a temporary cast was placed on my broken wrist because surgery wouldn't be available until the next night. As much as it sucked, I laid in bed all night with minimal pain medication. My wrist was throbbing. I was in tears, yet I endured. I couldn't sleep. Any time I tried to move an intense pain shot through my arm. The next day my parents made me go to school. I had to take a writing test with my opposite arm. And of course, the assholes that kids are, they'd slap the cast trying to get me to squirm. Writing this, I cannot express the amount of agony I was in throughout the day. I made it to surgery that night and woke to a real cast plastered on my arm. The doc prescribed better pain medication. At last the pain had subsided. The suffering was over, but it, like all these other experiences, built upon the sort of man I'd develop into, with the ability to bite down and press forward.

Along with my perseverance I also had a strong urge to help others as a child, partly because of my mother's big heart. She made sure we never looked down upon others and taught us to appreciate every luxury we were given. We were lucky to have what they provided when others had less. I'd tell my brother, "I wish I could carry the burden of all the people suffering from ailments, cancers and other hardships so that they don't have to." I wished I could steal away their anguish or sorrow so they could smile, even if only briefly. In my head and heart I was strong enough to carry the weight of the world. Many times, I'd stay up at night thinking of ways to ease human suffering, even contemplating throwing my hat into politics to make a real difference. I wrote in my journal about ushering in a time of happiness in the world where no one would have to worry about anything. Even when things were hard for me I knew there were countless people in the world going through something worse.

It is crazy to think the words I was speaking and writing would eventually help cultivate the life I needed to not just survive, but thrive. The universe gave me what I asked for and in my lowest moments,

in my darkest hour, I would have to claw my way out
to become the person I hoped to inspire others to be.

A SHIFT IN THOUGHT

Is it poetry or music I express when I write? However you take it, let it influence your life. Stop sitting on your hands waiting for things to change, you are smart enough to do it. Use the power of your brain. So, why is it so hard for us to accept? That the world is a crazy place it doesn't care or respect? Death no longer rattles me because I have been programmed to think this way, unfortunately, the image in the media projects it every day. I know it's random, no pattern or form. Issues that seem to leave other people torn, seem to be from what I was born. I am no longer stressing about things I can't change, even the leaders of our country are only out for fame. So, who I am I supposed to look up to in times like these? Even the leaders of the church have mistaken wants for needs. So, I chose to believe in myself, even though I am not perfect. At least I know what is most important to me, and it has nothing to do with my status or money. It's about what can I do for you. Not what you can do for me. It's about cherishing every day that the sky is blue. We have to know that somewhere the sun isn't shining, somewhere a heart has turned cold from someone else's unkindness. We need a change now, it has to happen now. Today is the day the world's fate gets turned around. The power of one voice can get turned down, but voices together can reach souls that are bound.

WHERE IS THE NEAREST BATHROOM?

This chapter is not for the squeamish. Life did not spare me the circumstances so I won't spare you the details. If you've made it this far, you agreed to take this journey with me. There is a light at the end of the tunnel, I promise, but I couldn't skip over this part of my life.

I live with Crohn's disease. To say it's an unpleasant disease would be an understatement. For those unfamiliar with Crohn's, a fitting, albeit disgusting, description of this disease can be summed up like this: Imagine eating five-day-old convenient store sushi after having greasy Mexican food the day

before, then washing it down with whole milk despite
the fact that you're lactose intolerant. I always
wondered if it was some cruel curse for something I
did in a past life, karmic punishment for past wrongs.
I wouldn't wish it on my worst enemy. Although I'm
currently in remission, with only a few flare-ups a
year, writing some of my struggles with this disease
opens psychological wounds.

It was a day like any other. I was sitting on the
couch playing PlayStation, beating my brother in
NCAA Football. That's when it hit me out of
nowhere. I must have been around fourteen, but I can
recall the feeling vividly. A wave of heat came over my
body, intense cramps in my stomach began to develop,
followed by a rumble, as if I were about to explode.

I assumed it was the gas I got from eating dairy, a
common issue that comes with being lactose
intolerant. My mom would get on me for doing that
but come on, seriously, you can't have cereal without
milk. I tried to expel the pressure in my stomach

through flatulence, only then did I realize this was different. That was the first day I couldn't make it to the restroom. It was the first time Crohn's began to strip apart my dignity, slowly and painfully. This was a challenge I wasn't sure I could handle.

I began having to use the bathroom much more frequently. Now I'm not talking the average three times a day, but a ludicrous ten, sometimes fifteen, times a day. Eighteen trips to the bathroom were common at the absolute peak of when the disease was at its worst. Blood, mucus, and liquids I can't even identify, were common every single time I had a bowel movement.

This chapter is not for the squeamish. Life did not spare me the circumstances so I won't spare you the details. If you've made it this far, you agreed to take this journey with me. There is a light at the end of the tunnel, I promise, but I couldn't skip over this part of my life.

I live with Crohn's disease. To say it's an

unpleasant disease to have would an understatement. For those unfamiliar with Crohn's, a fitting, albeit disgusting, description of this disease can be summed up like this: Imagine eating five-day-old convenient store sushi after having greasy Mexican food the day before, then washing it down with whole milk despite the fact that you're lactose intolerant. I always wondered if it was some cruel curse for something I did in a past life, karmic punishment for past wrongs. I wouldn't wish it on my worst enemy. Although I'm currently in remission, with only a few flare-ups a year, writing some of my struggles with this disease opens psychological wounds.

It was a day like any other. I was sitting on the couch playing PlayStation, beating my brother in NCAA Football. That's when it hit me out of nowhere. I must have been around fourteen, but I can recall the feeling vividly. A wave of heat came over my body, intense cramps in my stomach began to develop, followed by a rumble, as if I were about to explode.

I assumed it was the gas I got from eating dairy, a common issue that comes with being lactose intolerant. My mom would get on me for doing that but come on, seriously, you can't have cereal without milk. I tried to expel the pressure in my stomach through flatulence, only then did I realize this was different. That was the first day I couldn't make it to the restroom. It was the first time Crohn's began to strip apart my dignity, slowly and painfully. This was a challenge I wasn't sure I could handle.

I began having to use the bathroom much more frequently. Now I'm not talking the average three times a day, but a ludicrous ten, sometimes fifteen, times a day. Eighteen trips to the bathroom were common at the absolute peak of when the disease was at its worst. Blood, mucus, and liquids I can't even identify, were common every single time I had a bowel movement.

Imagine being a teenager and having this problem. The embarrassing number of times I had to ask permission to use the restroom at school. I had this burden to deal with at the same time I should be flirting with girls and being around friends. Imagine locker rooms full of ruthless teens and the sounds that came out of the stalls in the gym bathrooms. I lived with the reality that I was the last stop on my bus route. Every day with this disease was a battle of finding the nearest bathroom or thinking maybe I shouldn't eat because it might cause my stomach more discomfort. I had no clue what was wrong, I just knew my new normal was far from that.

One year, on the last day of school, I was extremely excited to start summer off with a bang. I was heading home talking to the bus driver when it hit, catching me off guard. An intense wave hit my stomach as if it were the first day all over again. I had to go. No amount of clenching or placating my thoughts would get me through it. Usually, mental processes bought me a little more time. But not that day. I sat down in my seat and, as discreetly as possible, while struggling to hold it in, I went. The floodgates opened, and there was nothing I could do to stop it. On top of it all, there were several witnesses, including a girl that I had a major crush on. I had no choice. With ten more minutes of the bus ride, I had to sit in what was the most odiferous crap you can imagine.

I was considerably lucky no one seemed to notice the smell was coming from me. The bus driver and other kids continued to comment on the stench but attributed it to someone having let some gas slip. I want you to close your eyes and really think about that, a kid surrounded by his peers sitting is his own filth, hoping with all hope no one would catch on and know it was me. Imagine shitting yourself on the bus that day. Replay the image in your head one more time and put yourself in my shoes.

When we arrived at my stop, I stood up and awkwardly departed. My sole focus was getting out the door. I glanced back at the seat to spy the remnants of fluid that had seeped through my blue jeans. I knew it would become someone else's problem to clean up but, at that point, it didn't matter. The damage was done. I didn't say goodbye to friends, I even ignored the bus driver's well wishes for summer. As I walked down my long rocky driveway, the tears welled up in my eyes, the wind hit my wet jeans, and I died inside. Talk about the ultimate embarrassment. It was rock bottom for a teenager. I had never felt so low. I took a long shower, closed the door to my room, and slept the whole night. A cloud of depression began to form around me.

I hid that disease from the world for a long time. I'm sure some of you are reading this and scolding me for not seeking medical attention. I never told my parents, hell, I never shared it with anyone. I never tipped my hand by mentioning it. I was just too embarrassed and didn't want to be a burden. I thought, if I could ignore it then the problem didn't really exist, or hopefully it would just go away.

I developed a routine to buffer the sounds coming from the bathroom. I'd turn on the shower, turn on the sink, and flush the toilet every time a wave hit my stomach. It was my new normal. As crazy as this is going to sound, part of me felt it was deserved. I don't know why, but honestly, that's what I believed.

I would go anywhere I could to avoid having another accident. I spent year after year continuously using nasty restrooms during long drives or stopping at fast food places, clenching all the way into the bathroom. If there wasn't toilet paper in the stall I couldn't try and hold it. That wasn't an option. There was no way I could make it to the next stop with clean underwear. And of course there was the constant concern someone would enter the bathroom and hear my body making its repulsive noises. I can't count how many times people came in and snickered at the sounds they heard. Little did they know the physical and mental torment I endured on the other side of those stall doors.

At home, my room was my safe space. Our house had two bathrooms, one in my parent's room, and the bathroom I shared with my older brother. I rarely used my parents' bathroom if they were home. Many close encounters involved waiting for my my brother to finish one of his long showers. On one such occasion, as I suffered a particularly rough episode, I banged on the door, begging and pleading to use the bathroom. My brother, not knowing the severity of the situation or even what I was going through day in and day out, ignored my request. I made a conscious decision that I would have to use my room. There was no way around it. I rushed to the linen closet and grabbed a towel. I slammed my door, hovered over the towel, and lost another piece of my soul that day. Although it felt good to relieve myself, it was just another blow to my teenage ego. It also meant another night spent crying myself to sleep.

Hope you're still with me because it gets worse.

Now, normally schools require each student to

ask to use the bathroom before being allowed to leave the classroom; the public school system's procedural lack of trust in kids and their need to be in total control of every child's movement. A teacher would either yay or nay your bathroom trip depending on the teacher's mood that day. To most students it was a minor nuisance, but one that didn't cause any major damage. For me and my uncontrollable bowels, this policy was a death sentence.

An episode struck in the middle of a test one day. I raised my hand and asked if I could use the restroom. The teacher turned down my request with the excuse that I might use it as an opportunity to cheat. I knew there was no way I could hold it for that long, trying to divide my focus on my stomach and test simultaneously. Once my body decided it needed to go there was just no stopping it. I was caught between a rock and a hard place. Faced with the chance of failing if I couldn't muster up the will to suppress it and, as a result, the wrath of my parents, I chose to fight the good fight and hold it. Let me tell you, it was the worst decision I could have made in that situation. The urge was too much to handle. I messed myself right there in the middle of class. I rushed to the teacher's desk, turned in my unfinished test and ran to the bathroom. The damage was done.

I sat in the bathroom stall that day, trying to decide what my next steps were going to be. I could leave school and never come back (typical dramatic teenage thinking), or I could clean up and make it appear as if nothing happened. I was unsure how much the other students had witnessed despite my quickly leaving the classroom. I ultimately decided it was a problem I could fix.

I grabbed as many paper towels as possible, doffed my clothes, and put a trashcan in front of the bathroom door to barricade myself in. I began to wash myself off in the sink. I trashed my underwear, poured pink soap everywhere, and scrubbed my bottom with fierce disgust. I scrubbed and scrubbed, trying hard to clean the incident away, physically and emotionally. Once my jeans were as clean as I could get them, I sat in front of the air dryer attempting to remove the wet stain on the back. I fully expected the teacher to check on me, or another student to come barging in. Maybe a janitor might come to restock supplies and catch me? Fortunately none of these possibilities happened though. After about twenty minutes of drying and praying, I returned to class.

I didn't make eye contact or speak to anyone. I smelled decent enough but I'm certain the other kids noticed. There was no way they could ignore the stench of pink soap and lingering scent. On that day, in that moment, the thought of ending my life crept into my mind. I knew I didn't have the balls to go through with suicide, but I couldn't stop playing the image over in my head. No one ever spoke of that day. This is the first time I have shared the story with anyone.

It's a funny thing how faith works when you're in

a situation like this. I prayed everyday, bargaining with God to improve my situation. I swore I'd read the Bible every day, never lie, or commit any other sin, just for an ounce of relief that never came. I no longer looked to Him for anything. I lost my faith, something I still struggle with now. Day after day, year after year, I fought these two battles alone. Over time I became calloused to the whole thing. I not only lost my faith, but I also lost belief in everything good. It was me against the world. If I could deal with this, there was nothing I couldn't get through. Rebellion became my first, middle and last name.

As my attitude gradually changed, I was also building a sense of inner strength and self reliance. There's something to be said for the tenacity a person can develop when against a challenge of this magnitude. I found resolve in believing anyone else would fold under similar circumstances. My days started with this thought in my head. How many people could do what I was doing? Who else could perform as a high-level athlete while being anemic from daily blood loss? How many people could navigate this disease, the exhaustion it caused, and still manage a facade of normalcy? I turned pain and embarrassment into motivational fuel.

I got through each day living with Crohn's disease by reciting this outlook any time I felt brought down by it. In turn, the trivial problems my peers dealt with became humorous to me. I started to foster a considerable chip on my shoulder. *Look at her complaining about her parents not letting her go to a party while I am over here corroding away internally. Oh, you got broken up with today? Well, I am too weak and exhausted to do anything besides sleep when I get home from school. Who are you? What makes you think you are better than me?* Nothing could make me feel any worse than the pain my own body was causing me. I never complained, I just put my head down and sucked it up. I didn't know if beating this thing was possible, but I knew I'd have to restructure my life or else it would destroy me.

Even though I was building up my resilience, the conflict between the devil and angel on opposing shoulders continued on. I still struggled with negative thoughts. I spent many nights wondering about my future with Crohn's. Would I ever be normal again? What girl, in her right mind, would accept a man as disgusting as me? How would I maintain a job when I spent so much time in the bathroom?

The anemia, caused by my Crohn's disease, continued to worsen until even a few steps to the mailbox made me dizzy and weak. My coaches noticed my performance slipping and I began to lose playing time. I went from an all-conference athlete to struggling to keep my starting position in a year's time. It got so bad that I couldn't stay hydrated due to the electrolytes I lost daily. My body was wracked by debilitating cramps during practice and during games. Since I kept everyone in the dark about my disesase, they just assumed I wasn't taking the necessary steps to prepare. There was no longer a youthful glow to my skin, instead I constantly looked stressed, sickly and weak. I was withering away.

I desperately needed something to help manage the depression I was sinking into. I turned to chemicals for respite. Huffing chemicals became my drug of choice and a long-time addiction. It contributed to my memory loss but it also helped me cope. It was the start of a dangerous decline. With the potential to kill, I don't think huffing gets the full attention it deserves.

In retrospect, I should have walked into my parents' room and told them the truth, the agony I was going through. The right choice is always so much clearer in hindsight. They would have gotten me the help that I needed and been there to share my burden. While a substantial number of people take medicine for Crohn's disease and still have symptoms, I could have at least gone into remission with proper medication sooner if I had spoken up earlier. Yet, I didn't take that route, and I can't fully regret the path

I chose since that experience, my lonely fight with Crohn's disease, contributed to the content of my character. I would not be who I am if I had not faced the Crohn's demon on my own. For all my stumbles, this disease had given me autonomy and fortitude

CHEMICALLY ALTERED

Everyone has used a cleaning product some time or another. Most of us know about the warnings on the back, the kind telling you inhaling these chemicals has the potential to cause brain damage, respiratory issues, or even sudden death. A rational person understands it's not in their best interest to expose themselves to chemicals intentionally in high volumes. Common sense, right? But because Crohn's had weakened my mental well-being I wasn't thinking rationally. There was a point in my life when I stooped so low as to find comfort in using these chemicals to alter my state of mind.

I had always enjoyed the unique aroma of cleaning chemicals but never in excess. While doing some hardcore spring cleaning in the bathroom, I sprayed the shower with bleach cleaner and poured Pine-Sol everywhere. The intent being for it to soak in and break through the grime and dirt. As the fumes permeated the room I intentionally turned the bathroom fan off for maximum inhalation. My eyes and chest began to burn as I took deep breaths.

I heard about getting high before but that was the first time I actually got high myself. As I was there, my mind began to change. The longer I waited to clean the shower, the more I took in these toxic fumes. Calmness washed over me. My mind relaxed and left my body. I was drifting away with each breath, all of my anguish- my secret, the personal shame, the negative toll it took on my mind, the physical pain-started to fade away. For the first time, something had finally alleviated my torture. I'll never forget that road marker in my life so well. It was the day I began a new fight, an intense battle, with addiction.

I went from abusing chemicals while cleaning to

doing it on a regular basis. I started wasting afternoons in my safe place when school and sports had finished. The bottle at my nose, I would take deep breaths in and out. I'd zone out to the fumes, music playing in the background, eyes glossed over, and my thoughts flatlining. That was coping, and I loved it.

The list of chemicals was quite extensive with favorites like Pine-Sol, gasoline, paint thinner, and even rubber cement from art class. If you could get high from it, I was going to huff it. Whenever I had a rough day from Crohn's, or just couldn't cope, I'd soak a rag in chemicals and put it to my nose. If I was on punishment, I turned to chemicals. If I was in a socially awkward situation, you guessed it, chemicals. I could forget my troubles. Nothing could hurt me while I was under. I didn't care that the side effects of my abuse were starting to show. As you might expect, I did a good job of hiding it from everyone. It's not something I'm proud to admit.

Allow me to talk briefly about the effects of this

habit. I spent many days with headaches and chest pain. Other times I couldn't get my nose to stop bleeding. The outer skin of my nose was so dry and chemically burned I had to apply Vaseline to dull the micro-adhesions created. The chemical haze, on top of the anemia from my illness, made me extremely tired most days. It was commonplace for me to come home from school and nap until dinner. That meant disregarding my homework, going back to bed after eating, and repeating the deadly cycle the next day. I often slept a whole weekend without anyone knowing why I was always so tired. Although sniffing chemicals numbed my pain, I was inviting a more threatening cloud over my life. It would take a near-death experience to pull me out of this desperate situation.

There were other options that would have been just as effective. Marijuana comes to mind. It wouldn't have been hard to get a hook up at school. I tried smoking and even prescription pills a few times. Nothing quite measured up to the feeling of huffing chemicals. Drugs couldn't compare to the feeling of those vapors going straight to my brain. Not to mention, it conveniently easy to hide. You can't pull out a joint and smoke in any situation, but I could pull out a doused rag and innocently pretend to wipe my nose. I could do that anywhere, anytime, and nobody questioned me about it.

Of course, I had some reservations about my lifestyle. Especially because at the time my school was running a solid anti-huffing campaign. I can faintly recall a few TV commercials discussing the potential for teenagers to develop addictions like mine. I was the kid in those commercials, crying out for help, slowly killing myself. I knew the harm it was causing but the reward was well worth the risk.

I shrugged it off because I convinced myself I was in total control and could stop at any time. I failed several times at doing just that. A few days passed and I would tell myself I was done playing the game of Russian roulette with my brain. There was a correlation between my worst Crohn's days and relapsing. I caved, so easily and often gave into my despair. That moment eventually came and almost cost me my life.

I don't remember what drove me to the edge that day. What I do remember is that I wanted to end it all, not to dull my suffering again and again, but to completely erase it from existence. I decided the only way out was to end my life.

The situation was taking a heavy toll on me. The huffing turned me irrational and the normal problems of a teenage life weighed heavily on my heart. I had enough of the world. I was done with the struggle. I grabbed some paint thinner, Pine-Sol, and a rag presoaked with gasoline. My parents were at work. I knew I couldn't do it without music in the background to drown out the voices in my head. So, I turned the radio up as loud as it could go.

I locked the door and slid a towel underneath then walked to the bathtub and poured in an entire bottle of Pine-Sol, mixed with some paint thinner to intensify the vapors. I poured the same mixture into the sink. I turned on the shower to create a steaming miasma and lowered myself next to the tub. My head was hovering above the mixture but it wasn't enough. I put the bottle of paint thinner under my nose, along with the rag soaked with gasoline. My plan was to inhale enough to pass out and end it. I certainly had enough artillery to do the job. My mind brought up reflections of those I would miss although I wasn't sure they'd miss me. I slumped onto the floor, no more than five minutes into it, with one last deep inhale. What happened next still remains unclear to me.

Something saved my life that day. I can't remember getting up on my own or being picked up off the floor by another. Yet somehow I found myself in bed looking at the alarm clock in the middle of the night. I sat up, confused and without a sense of where I was and why. I made it out somehow, some way. Could it have been a guardian angel that saved my life, or was I too high to remember getting up off the floor? It happened. I went through with it. The evidence was there. The bathroom was free of chemicals and the used bottles were in the trashcan. They were proof I hadn't been dreaming. This wasn't a concoction of my imagination. Although I couldn't recall the events, one thing was clear. I had a serious problem and I needed help.

I don't want to cast total blame on my disease. It's not a scapegoat. I admit I was responsible for harm I was inflicting on my body. I'm accountable for this addiction. Because I held myself accountable, I looked inward for strength. Sure, there were resources out there for people like me, and my family would have made sure I got the help that I needed. The few friends I had would surely sympathize and be there to lend a helping hand. But I've always been strong willed and hard headed. I knew the solution I needed would come from within myself.

The day after my suicide attempt, I went back to

the bathroom and had a reality check in the mirror. Looking at myself there, I hated the person staring back, how weak I had become. I let all these issues take complete control of my actions and reasoning. I needed to change. I told myself I'd never again touch a chemical product with the intent of getting high. I'd never let a thing as petty as addiction control my life, and no matter how bad life got, suicide would never be an option again. That was when I developed the, *embrace the suck*, motto.

Yes, there are still days when I feel like the person I was that day on the bathroom floor. I find it difficult to use cleaners or walk down the cleaning aisle at the grocery store. I will never be able to use a cleaner that smells like pine again. I have a strange salivating experience every time I pump gas. I grow upon the pain of a challenge. I tackle difficulties and face any obstacles that come my way. That's what it is to embrace the suck. Taking a negative that defeats others and coming out more resilient from the experience out of sheer willpower. The hard path builds character.

I've come to learn that with every hardship comes a valuable lesson. There are those out there dealing with crippling and destructive addictions. Alcohol, recreational drugs, and gambling can take control of life and slowly kill them. People think their self-worth is of little to no value. But I promise you can come out on the other side. Your method doesn't have to mirror mine. You might need rehab or therapy to kick your addiction, there is no shame in that, in getting help. But in order to make a change for the better, you have to start building the life you want for yourself, a day at a time.

I can tell you my method, embracing the suck, helped me through tough times. Of course even after overcoming my hurdles and finding the right path to take, there would be new trials to face. The experiences of your past are but small hills compared to the mountains you climb later in life, when our choices become more permanent. My next challenge would be joining the United States Army. Nothing could prepare me for the experiences the Army would put me through.

A L T E R E D

No words can be said, no action can be taken, there is no coming back from mistakes I've been making. My life has become one of declination, I give up I give in to the BS that I am facing. As the wind hits my face, I hear screams from below. For sure this will be my last step then I am gone. Last breath that I am blowing, last sight I am beholding, but I pause for the now to leave the world my poem. Is the world ready for something this real they have to know it, is anyone going to remember this dead poet? So many years of pain held inside I didn't show it, built up in me now from a pen it starts flowing. I've kept holding on, showing positivity through negative scenes the world has been showing. It's getting impossible to stop my thoughts and save a life, I have to make a change on my own.

THE LIGHTER SIDE OF THE

ARMY:

YOU WANT ME TO DO WHAT?

That was a lot to unpack. Let's lighten the mood for a moment. I promised there'd be some laughs and I've yet to deliver.

I've been often complimented on my patience and even-keeled temperament. The time I spent in the Army was at times humorous but also tested that patience. It should go without saying, the military is not an easy endeavor. Drill sergeants yelling during basic training, handling weapons, and dealing with deployments barely begins to skim the surface. Those were part of my seven and a half years in the Army. I spent a good portion of my career with a puzzled look on my face. There were moments in the military so ludicrous they drove me to question my actual purpose on this planet.

I was placed in rear detachment when I arrived to my unit. The unit was filled with soldiers that did not deploy with the rest of the unit for various reasons. Some were pending disciplinary action, had babies on the way, or had serious health concerns. The bulk of rear detachment was new to the unit like me. As we waited for the unit to return, we conducted training, with the idea that through training we'd play catch up with those deployed. Our sergeants led classes in weapons training, deployment classes, and basic army readiness. However, my first task in this unit, as a new soldier, was to pick dandelions out of the long field in the front of our buildings. You read that right. Dandelions.

It was a yard the size of half a football field, filled with hundreds of harmless dandelions, a sea of yellow.

Apparently, those in charge thought these weeds were an eyesore to the rest of the post. One of my sergeants placed me on a five-man detail to eliminate them. The repercussions for him seeing any yellow at the end of the day would be a good smoke session, as the Army calls it. Smoking involves an ungodly number of push-ups and character building shouts. No, we couldn't just mow them down with a lawnmower. No, we couldn't wait until the cold weather of Washington State killed them off. We couldn't pretend they didn't exist. We spent the whole day picking them out of the ground and putting them in trash bags. All that work because one man much higher up on the military food chain, a sergeant major, found the sight of them insulting. In the Army we call it "area beautification".

Now, I am all for area beautification. You might recall me mentioning the yard work I'd already done in my life. I knew part of being in the military required a certain level of discipline and pride in your living space. My unit was deployed in Iraq and I'd be joining them in less than a month. Yet, there I was on rear detachment picking dandelions. I couldn't fathom it. I was so wet behind the ears that I could barely shoot a weapon, learning that skill seemed way more important. At least that could save my life. This was just a waste of time. I barely had any equipment at that point. Yet none of that was nearly as vital as picking those dandelions.

There were no words of gratitude when the task was done. I realized gratitude would be scarce in the military, which always seemed like a slap in the face because I was raised with manners. I was raised to say thank you. As anyone could predict, two weeks later, the dandelions returned. Our leaders assembled another five-man detail to reenact the same menial task. It's a damn shame I missed out on that detail.

The area where I lived was the oldest on base. The buildings were so dated they still had old coiled heaters with large knobs in every room, and most of the knobs were so rusted that they were impossible to turn. This meant in the winter the barracks felt more like a meat locker than a place to live. Several barracks buildings were posted with signs that read, "CONDEMNED," due to asbestos or another health and safety concern. They were too derelict to house people. Our superiors continued to make empty promises of moving us to better locations, I think for the sake of morale. A few were scheduled to be torn down, replaced, or refurbished in the coming months.

You can imagine my shock one morning when the platoon sergeant asked for a detail to paint one of these old buildings. Our sergeant major would be coming to inspect our work. We had to paint the walls and scrub off the scuff marks and imperfections from years and years of neglect. I never volunteered for these sorts of details. Instead I was volunteered against my will, volun-*told*, another word familiar to those who've served. Low ranking troops were volun-told first, per usual. I mustered up the resolve to not to air my complaints. I was just a private and any pushback would've ended with me in the push-up position getting yelled at.

Six of us went into the vacant building with brushes and gallons of paint under our arms and spent the next three days painting and scrubbing the walls. The building was unoccupied so I can only assume we were preparing it for the ghost of soldiers past. When we were done, not a single thanks or further explanation was given. I don't even know if the sergeant major ever inspected our work. It turned out to be another unnecessary task to complete. What I do know, is about a month later, that building was completely condemned. The newly painted walls never saw the light of day. My sweat equity is stored somewhere, waiting for some appreciation that at this point will never come.

I have countless experiences in the military like that, lots of sitting around all day with nothing to do. We'd shoot the breeze waiting until five o'clock (1700 military time) closing formation when a higher-ranking soldier would release us for the evening. And there, so close to freedom, someone would walk out of the office screaming there were more menial tasks to complete. That meant another pointless long night. It meant more time away from family or other things you enjoyed.

There were early morning training sessions freezing outside when we had to run in thirty-degree freezing rain, with minimum coverage. I still think days like that were strictly meant for torture and control. The Army isn't short on sadistic leaders who'd rather spend time at work than at home. Might explain why the divorce rate is so high in the military.

Picture this, like any company or business, the army consolidates all its valuable items. Included among the most prized objects are random items-outdated, broken, or cheap- ultimately useless and taking up unnecessary space. They place it all in impenetrable and nigh impregnable metal container then set it inside a secured fence, where only a select few have access. We took inventory of that container weekly, even though it was never moved or opened. Everything was laid out and counted individually while we waited hours for an NCO or platoon leader to casually verify our count.

We had to start inventory at a specific time, everything laid out "dress right dress" or heads would roll. Every single time, the superior would show up hours late. While we waited, at least one person had to pull guard duty. After all, someone might steal it, right? Plenty of this equipment requires two men or more to move it, but you never know. We did that multiple times per day sometimes. If our superior missed something during the chaos then we had to start all over.

I have stories of being deployed in a combat zone...picking weeds. According to our first sergeant, picking weeds would help the random cat on the Iraqi base catch field mice. The one cat in all of Iraq, at least the only one I ever saw. The mice ate through our care packages at night. Our orders were to pick weeds so the cat could chase the mice. This was combat? What was happening? I always put my head down and did what was asked, but boy was I screaming internally!

Until recently, I never understood what all those ridiculous moments taught me. The Army taught me to endure the monotonous and insignificant aspects of life better than anyone or anything I know. Do you have to wait in a long line? Most people complain, I just get lost in my thoughts and endure. Is it freezing outside or raining like the world is ending? Well, I can endure that too, without even a bit of discomfort. Haven't eaten all day, slept, and no break in sight? Well, I've gone complete twenty-four hour days without food or sleep.

Consider a situation you in which you might complain about something insignificant. Stop. Take a moment and stop complaining. There are people going through much worse every day. With the ease of today's conveniences, most of our problems are trivial. I learned to overlook the little annoyances when life in the Army put me up against real problems.

Those moments taught me immense patience. I owe a great part of my character to them. There were plenty more serious times throughout my Army career as well. I'm still jaded about the time spent away from my family and friends. I served from the age of seventeen to twenty-five. Although some of the changes were for the better, I don't completely understand how everything affected me. Yet, it is my hope those who often tell me I'm a government programmed robot, might realize there's a little more complexity to it.

JANUARY 18ᵀᴴ, 2007

People have been saying I don't smile much lately. I tell them I save those expressions for moments when I am truly happy...

SO YOU WANT TO JOIN THE

ARMY?

My parents will give you a different story as to why I joined the military. According to their version of events, they offered to help pay for college and offered me a living space until I figured out what I wanted to do. But I declined their help and in a rebellious fit joined the army. I remember it differently. I remember struggling through high school with average grades and average effort. I focused more on surviving my ailments, not passing standardized tests. Sports and popularity also took precedence over grades. I read college brochures and heard about friends being accepted into their schools of choice. I did want to go to college, if I remember correctly, I just didn't have the finances to do so. Average grades meant I needed college loans and incur the same debt plaguing half the country.

I wanted to attend college on the West Coast, rent a studio apartment in California or somewhere far away from home. Maybe volunteer in the peace corps or just party it up and meet new people and have new experiences. I wanted to rebuild myself and get away from everything in that small town and the negative sentiment I had for it. Everything was pushing me to leave the house. Be independent. In a last-ditch effort, I joined the military. Felt like I had no other options. Perhaps my parents are right and I've lied to myself all these years to justify a decision that heavily impacted the course of my life. Maybe I don't want to claim that decision as my own. Maybe it was the best decision I could have made at the time, given my circumstances. Whatver the case may be, the summer after I graduated high school, at the age of seventeen, I went off to basic training. June 30th,

2005.

I shipped off to Fort Leonard Wood, in Missouri. I was nervous but ready to tackle nine weeks of intense training. America's toughest boot camp! Prior to joining, I had taken time to watch the videos and heard stories from my recruiters, but I wanted to see for myself what the hype was all about. I was just a kid and still so naïve about the world. Everyone at basic training was much older than me and must have viewed me as a scared puppy. I was totally out of my element. My friends were off growing up, partying, and making young mistakes, and there I was becoming a hardened, structured, soldier.

I'd come home on leave and hang with my old friends. They'd tell me tales about crazy parties and insanely wild spring break. Each stayed in contact with one another and created new relationships. I had nothing to compare. Here I was, just a boy amongst grown men, men with vastly more experience than I. How could I ever bond with them? It was such a different way of life, I couldn't explain these experiences to my friends. What could I talk about, getting screamed at for messing up a direct order? Would I tell them about taking inventory or learning to shoot a rifle? That I wasn't allowed to talk while eating, or that I had to stand in a line with my tray and head facing forward at lunchtime, just like a prison. I could tell them how I had two minutes to scarf down as much food as I could without making a peep. If I made any noise while eating, a drill sergeant would flip my tray and foam at the mouth while screaming at me to do push-ups.

I was jealous. In fact, I'm still quite jealous. Everyone should be able to experience those formative years of living a little recklessly, having carefree fun, and learning about oneself. That's true independence. Life comes in stages, and I, unfortunately, skipped that stage. I matured too early and lost my sense of youthful playfulness. With being a soldier I had to carry the burden of responsibilities.

Would I do it all over again? I hated almost every bit of my time in the military, although there were days I briefly enjoyed myself. There were mornings I'd cry while driving through the gate for work, miserable about the day that lay ahead, full of pointless tasks to accomplish. I spent one depressing holiday after another alone in my cold barracks room. There were times I had the opportunity to party and make mistakes like my peers back home. None of it felt like what I imagined life would be like for me back in North Carolina.

There were instances I faced disciplinary actions for physically and verbally lashing out at someone. I harbored regret and anger for my decision to join and took it out on those around me. I'd decline any invitations to barracks parties or get-togethers from my buddies. Occasionally, I formed a bond with a fellow soldier. My barracks room was my new safe place. Alone in my room was where I felt the most comfortable.

My kidneys were destroyed by dehydration during long missions. I've been diagnosed with stage three kidney disease. The doctor says I will eventually need dialysis or a transplant. I will outlive my kidneys. I blame the long deployments in the sandbox and the temperatures over 100°.

I'm one of the few people that deleted every picture I had from my time in the military. One day I'll explain to my children that their father did in fact serve. I was deployed, despite having no photographic evidence as proof. I didn't keep my uniforms or medals. I had no desire to relive those memories and rarely talked about them. I dissociated myself from online military groups and friends I served with to avoid a trip down memory lane.

The craziest part is, I would do it all again.

Even though I despised taking commands everyday for over seven years, I owe the military a debt of thanks. I owe it for maturing my mindset and giving me some needed structure. It put me in the toughest positions you could imagine and didn't allow me to quit until I accomplished the goal. I learned to better communicate with people. It taught me to accept myself. I became a man faster in the Army than I would have going to college.

I'd eventually come out of my shell and meet some amazing people along the way. I had a chance to go up and down the West Coast. I visited Canada often and even partied down in Mexico when I shouldn't have. I swapped stories with Ugandan soldiers and ate bread while drinking chai tea with Iraqis. I was a part of history serving this country during my deployment. None of my friends in college would ever have those experiences. They were earning a piece of paper while I was earning real life knowledge. What I did was rare, only a small percent join. Most people don't have the discipline to be a soldier. I sincerely carry a sense of pride when I tell someone that I served. So, hell yes, I would do it all over again.

Do I recommend someone join the military? Honestly, no. It turned out perfect for me but it's not for everyone. Go to school or get a regular job until you figure things out, where you want to go in life. Experience youth without someone structuring the entire day for you. Experience traveling without restriction. If the physicality of the job seems enticing, may I suggest doing it on your own without taking on the punishing demands of the military. Time spent away from family is difficult. I deployed to Iraq twice, a total of twenty-seven months and barely a year between each to catch a breath. It felt like I barely got home and it was time to ship out again.

I missed the birth of my first child, the first year of his life. There's a connection to him from that time I've struggled to build. Relationships with cousins, aunts, uncles and even immediate family have suffered because of my absence. I wake up screaming from nightmares. People ask me why I don't like holidays, it's because I missed so many of them being in a different state or country. Or why I don't call or reach out frequently. I went months without any contact from family on several occasions. No one's life stopped for mine. The pop of a champagne cork caught me off guard recently. It reminded me of Iraq and I started to cry. But these are some of the reasons for the anger and resentment I feel towards my service while at the same time I take immense pride in it. It's not as black and white as it may seem.

Reflecting on those seven years has become important to me now that I've aged. No one knows what I truly went through during those years. I'll likely never be comfortable talking about certain events that unfolded during my time in. You can't truly appreciate the sacrifice of service unless you have served yourself. As cliché as it sounds, it's sadly true, though I wish it could be different. The military life is unlike any other and while it built me up in certain ways, it tore me down in others.

THOUGHTS IN BASIC

TRAINING

I am living a nightmare, like young kids watching Halloween flicks. I just can't shake the images I awake to, it's the same world I close my eyes and leave yet return to every day. The only difference this day is how I will fare. Some days are positive but always with negativity hanging overhead. I can't shake this curse, my new home away from home. Thinking about goals I won't be able to accomplish, to hit them now would only encompass three more years of struggle. I must endeavor. I ask myself daily why I chose this route? Who cares, it's just another day of my life wasted.

18 HOURS IN HELL

I'm not one to tell war stories like soldiers whose accomplishments revolve solely around their military service. We all know people embellish stories and claim everything on the backbone of their own personal efforts. There are soldiers that leech off any discount or benefit they can get their hands on. I call bullshit in my head when I hear unrealistic and obviously inflated war stories. The most braggadocios person usually has no reason to be, but I've never been one to call people out. And of course this doesn't include those comfortable enough to share their very real stories. It's just not my thing.

Iraq can be scorching. It's almost indescribable how hot it gets there. Although the temperature easily exceeds 120° most days. Soldiers routinely wear around sixty pounds of armor which, combined with the long-sleeved uniform, traps body heat and can make Iraq feel like hell on earth. On top of that, we carry an assault rifle-sometimes a secondary weapon-and enough ammo for both in case of a lengthy bullet exchange, and grenades for the serious situations.

Through intense physical and mental training, soldiers are groomed for combat. Our suffocating thick boots and oversized Kevlar helmets, like all things in the military, serve a functional purpose in war. Being covered head to toe means being bogged down with such necessities. It takes a few months to become accustomed to the constant sweating, taking cold showers to cool down, and briefly enjoying moments of cool dryness before having to repeat the cycle. The one place that ever compared to Iraq was Fort Polk, Louisiana, in the dead summer, minus the aridity of the former. I spent some time training in the deep Louisiana bayou, and let's just say I'll never voluntarily return to that state.

During my first deployment, in 2007, my brigade was tasked with some of the hardest missions of any unit in that area. We were part of the heavy surge deployed to the most violent area of the Middle East, the Diyala province in eastern Iraq. It was the deadliest time during the war since the 2003 invasion. Our mission: to eliminate the growing threat of radical terrorists. These were terrorists who wired houses to blow up when soldiers entered them. Terrorists who planted bombs on their own roads in attempts to destroy our passing vehicles. Terrorists who had no reservations about killing civilians in the process. They were the types to strap bombs to kids or drive cars into crowded areas to elicit maximum chaos. All in the name of religion.

I remember laying in bed, relaxing from a hard week of missions inside the major cities in the area, when my sergeant came in with a new mission. In combat we're all in a state of readiness, so the spontaneity didn't catch me off guard in the slightest. Of course, we had no idea what was in store for us. All we had were our expectations and anticipations as our commander gave us the mission brief. There was a demobilized Blackhawk helicopter that had taken enemy gunfire. Mechanical issues caused them to make an emergency landing in the middle of a field. Our task would be to secure the area, surround the helicopter to prevent the enemy from stripping it down to the frame.

Priced around six-million dollars, a Blackhawk is an expensive piece of military equipment, so you can see the urgency in securing it. Iraqis would love to rip apart its contents to sell them or reassemble the parts to use against coalition forces. Another helicopter would drop our team at the location to hold and secure the wreckage while waiting for an available Chinook to come and retrieve it for repairs. According to the mission brief, it would take just a few hours to complete in what should have been relative safety. An

99

easy task, and on the surface it seemed like it was panning out to be one of our least intense missions. That couldn't have been further from the truth.

After preparation and a final rehearsal, our team loaded onto the Blackhawks with our weapons locked and loaded. *"Everything is good"*, I thought to myself as we disembarked. Things were pretty awesome. It was something straight out of a movie. I kept thinking we would have an amazing story to tell once the mission was complete. It was another scorcher outside, but as long as we didn't stay very long it would be bearable. As with every mission, we had water via CamelBaks and MREs. With food and water on hand, what could go wrong? It seemed we were completely ready to accomplish the task.

My adrenaline pumping, we surrounded the downed helicopter with plenty of space between the *bird* and ourselves, in case of an enemy mortar attack. Bunching up makes you an easier target. That was a big concern for our commanders. If the enemy knew

100

we arrived, they could locate our position and barrage us with mortars. That would have turned a decent day into an unpleasant one. And even though Iraqis were terrible shots, even a dead clock is right twice a day.

We started early to reduce the number of witnesses to our movement. The enemy sometimes had lookouts phone each other the direction we traveled. Our sole mission was to fan out and protect the Blackhawk if the enemy approached. Surprisingly, the enemy that day wasn't a terrorist but rather the blazing Iraqi heat. The first hours went by like a breeze. It was morning, the full strength of the sun had not come out. Adrenaline tends to mask discomfort. I also had the benefit of my water supply to quench my thirst.

We paired up to ensure that each of us was feeling okay or in case someone needed to eat an MRE all sectors of gunfire would remain covered. 360° of protection around the bird. No gaps. No deviations from the plan. A few more hours went by and that's when Iraq's sun began to take hold. Dehydration and heat stroke started to rear their ugly heads. Around the fifth hour of being out in the sun is when it really hit me hard.

In the haze of my memories, I recall seeing soldiers physically unable to muster the energy to pull security, not for lack of trying. If the enemy had attacked, there and then, it would have been a slaughter. Nobody was in any state of mind to fight back. I could feel my insides cooking from the heat. Eventually we started running low on water. Helicopters flew over to assist, dropping packages of water along with some IV bags. The problem is, at those temperatures- 120s-140s- it doesn't take long for water to become scalding. It was like water straight out of a boiling pot. I knew we were in serious trouble when people started passing out. As each one went down I felt myself start to slip.

The sun zapped all our energy. Nobody was alert or even seemed to care about the mission anymore.

The mission had changed to one of survival and I
made sure to check on my partner to keep us from
passing out. At some point, my eyes glossed over and I
lost track of time. I even started crying, not sobbing
tears, but steady drops that streamed down my cheek.
I was scared and miserable. The worst part was that I
felt myself drifting off and didn't know what to do.
Everyone was battling their own bodies to stay alive.
I've had the feeling of facing impending doom before,
normally it subsides as the threat disappears. This
threat seemed to last a lifetime. My mind started to
tell my body that I wouldn't make it.

Another part of the unit was supposed to pick us
up because they knew we wouldn't last much longer
out there. I remember a sergeant saying the *trucks*
were on their way to "save us". There was a moment
of internal jubilation at that announcement. It meant
we just had to hold on just a little longer. There was
hope. But the trucks never made it to our location.
While en route, our relief hit an IED that destroyed

an entire vehicle. It was in that catastrophe we lost a great soldier that day, someone who I had several impactful encounters with.

Out of respect to his platoon and family, I won't try to speak on the events that took place, because I don't know the full story. I wasn't there with them at that moment. Who knows, maybe someone who lived through that will share their story someday. That moment was bigger than any heat stroke or hot water we had to endure. It still haunts me. The only reason they hit that IED, on that day and on that route, was because they were headed to our location, to relieve us. In hindsight, I like to think we could have suffered longer, endured further, and maybe the outcome would have been different. Such contemplation hurts, and I will forever reflect on that day.

Once they announced we would stay out longer, I remember reflecting on specific moments of my life and all the things I'd previously gone through. I thought of the moments that were rough and how in those moments I was able to suck it up and keep going, pushing through my trials. It was what I always seemed to do in those situations. Now there I was, a soldier and a man. I was in phenomenal mental and physical shape to survive this ordeal as I did all others since. The resolve I found from that experienced inspired the message I teach to my clients and anyone who can benefit from hearing it.

We spent over eighteen hours on that mission. I don't remember if anyone fixed the helicopter, if it was lifted out, or if we just left it there. Almost a full day later, helicopters flew in and picked us up. There was no greater feeling than seeing those *birds* flying in. I don't remember anyone else's reaction, my brain was literally fried, but I speculate they felt the same. I used my last bit of energy to walk onto that helicopter and took a seat as we flew back to base. My health and a piece of my soul was left on that field in Iraq. I've always said if anyone happens to find it, keep it, because in losing it I built an even stronger resolve.

No one on my team died that day or was grievously injured, but we needed the next few days to recover from the damage the heat had inflicted. My body hurt all over. I needed two full IVs, meal after meal, and hibernation-like sleep. After a few days of recovery spent hardly moving, the medic checked on my team and deemed everyone fit to get back in the fight. Physically I was fine, but it had taken a strong mental toll on everyone. It almost felt like dying. There was resentment for being there and grief for the platoon that struck the IED. It put me in a very negative headspace. I've never been the same since, and I still don't know the full extent of the harm the sun might have inflicted on me in the long term. Already, some of these concerns are starting to manifest.

I've been wrestling with some very concerning health issues. I know that that mission is the reason for my health decline. The spiked blood pressure, headaches and intense nightmares, have all been the results of that day. During a routine checkup, it was discovered that I have stage three kidney disease. My kidneys are functioning with the efficiency of a senior citizen. I only have thirty percent function in both. This is an ailment that will change the rest of my life. I can't eat certain foods and I can never allow myself to get dehydrated. I also need to avoid stress, sick people or getting sick myself because it could put too much stress on my body and cause kidney failure. No average person the age of thirty wants or expects to be put on a kidney donor list. One day I could wake up extremely sick. From that moment forward, I'll need dialysis until I receive a transplant. These are, sometimes, the unglamorous repercussions of serving one's country.

LOSING A FRIEND

These tears are being shed for a worthy cause/I sit and pause thinking how I will endure this loss/there's nothing I can do, nothing I can say, if today were yesterday I wouldn't feel this way/the sounds of save me's remain upstairs/I am thinking about pay back but the world doesn't care/so why should I stand strong and not let emotions take over/ at what point does the enemy get left without a 4 leaf clover/ I hold back and sit in silence and remember our times/ even those little memories seem to replay in my mind/ All I can really say is I am missing you man/ you will be my motivation for turning my cants to cans.

THE MILITARY,

ON FAST-FORWARD

There a few more details about my time in the military I'd like to cover here. Memories come to me fast and then disappear. One such memory, from a different event, comes to mind and my thoughts shift to another point in time. My experience serving in the military is a huge part of who I am today. In basic training, there is a checklist of things to complete before being allowed to graduate. One of these checkmarks requires the daunting obstacle that is the NBC (nuclear, biological, and chemical) chamber, or gas chamber as some know it. Sounds scary right? It was for me.

I had to wear a complete chemical protection suit

with a gas mask in the middle of a Missouri summer. The mask made it hard to breathe. I had to walk inside a dark enclosed room full of CS gas, which I can only describe as a miasma of cayenne and chili peppers. The gas mask, in theory, was supposed to shield you from the chemicals and allow you to breathe. Again in theory, if the mask is properly sealed. Problem was, mine didn't seal. As soon as stepped foot into the chamber I took in the full potency of the CS gas. There was little I could do to amend the situation. The drill sergeants barricade the door as soon as you enter and you can't leave until you stay in there long enough to pass.

I started coughing before throwing up inside my mask. My face and eyes were burning. It was so deep in my lungs that I could only take shallow breaths. Everyone else seemed to be okay, their masks sealed properly. That was, until the drill sergeant ordered everyone to remove them to sing the alphabet. They found it humorous. There we were, everyone running around like chickens with their heads cut off.

One of the drill instructors kept hollering for me to calm down, but I couldn't. I ran to the door to get out, but he pushed me down on the ground. That was it. I was going to die. I scrambled to regain my composure. It seemed like the longest most torturous moment of my life until he opened the doors and we all ran out. I had snot pouring from my nose, the ultimate cure for congestion. I eventually recovered and a drill sergeant asked if I wanted to go through it again, to which I emphatically declined. I passed and did whatever I could to dodge having to do it ever again.

There were many new experiences during my first deployment, amongst them being the first time I was shot at. We were driving down the road and I was manning the vehicle's weapon, a .50 caliber machine gun beast. The rounds from this weapon could easily rend limbs, cut through the walls of a house, or penetrate another vehicle's armor. Out of the blue, I heard pinging on the side of our vehicle. One ping turned into a steady barrage. Multiple rounds landed a couple of feet my gun turret. A little too close for comfort.

My immediate reaction was anger. I took it so personally, I seriously contemplated why someone would shoot at us. The *truck* commander announced small arms contact. We were under fire from somewhere off in the distance. Whoever the shooter was, they exhibited very little proficiency or accuracy. I couldn't really pinpoint the source. My training took over. I whipped the .50 cal. around to where I suspected the shots originated from and laid on the trigger. I had no clue if I was hitting anything. It didn't matter. What mattered was that I returned fire. Whoever the guy was, he'd pay for shooting at me. After about thirty seconds of shared fire, I must have hit him or forced him to ceasefire. The shooting stopped.

It was the first, but definitely not the last time an

enemy shot at me. There were many other close calls but you never forget that first time. It also realized my training worked. Every drill we practiced had been committed to memory so completely, reaction became instinctive. I trusted these instincts. Repetition is a great way to build beneficial habits.

When you get back from a deployment, the military does its best to help you readjust to society. In America, you'd be put in jail if you did any of the things we had to do over there. In Iraq, we could drive on the wrong side of the road, enter nearly any building, and brazenly carry a weapon. It's the norm. Army deployments are usually over a year long. That's a year's worth of habits you needed to survive. Readjustment is harder than you might expect. A year of aggressive habits seem normal to us. And there's a rush there that you begin to miss. The Army give you opportunities to participate in some exhilarating activities to curb you aggression and satisfy the rush you lose coming back, with the hopes of keeping us

113

out of trouble and to feel a semblance of normalcy again. We could participate in speed paintball, skydiving, snowboarding, or bungee jumping. A few friends and I signed up for bungee jumping.

I volunteered for one of the most terrifying moments in my life. We drove to Mount St. Helens, in Washington State, to the location of one of North America's tallest bungee jump bridge. The jump was about 400-foot with freezing rapids and rocks below. I watched everyone strap up and handle things like a champ. Everyone was smiling when they came up, as if there was some prize at the bottom. I was happy they were having such a good time until my turn came up. I declined a few times, said I was going to sit it out. I was scared shitless.

I changed my mind when a girl who had just come back up from her jump mocked me and called me names. It was the spark I needed. I shook off the fear and headed to the platform. The instructors strapped me in as I approached the edge. My head was awash with thought. Why would I sign up for this? Who designed this as a "fun" activity? What if I don't go through with it? Despite my reservations, I knew there was only one way through it. I had to jump. With eyes closed, I counted to three and took my leap.

I screamed the entire descent. When I bounced at the end, what seemed only five feet from the water below, I hollered even more. By the time they pulled me up I was still hollering. Everyone was laughing at me for my hysterics, but I didn't care, I had done something I watched several people walk away from, something I almost did as well. It wasn't until afterwards, I realized there was something at the bottom- confidence. I felt, in that moment, the rush I had back in Iraq. I felt alive.

Sometimes you have to just jump. You can sit there and let the fear eat away at you until you eventually talk yourself down or you can take a leap of faith. When you push yourself beyond that fear you find a part of yourself you didn't know was there. If you don't, if you step down, you'll miss out on the experience. The reward of overcoming your fear. Even if other people are terrified, you can't allow it to stop. It's okay to have reservations, doubts, but there's something beautiful and valuable in diving headfirst into that unknown. I was so close to missing out on discovering this new side of me and my potential. Fortunately, I took advantage of that opportunity and can say I've bungee jumped from one of the tallest sites in the United States, something few others have ever even attempted.

Those who know me or have at least seen me would say that I am in phenomenal shape. I don't say that to brag. I've spent years and years working on my fitness. It's a strength of mine as well as my profession, but in basic training I sucked. It wasn't the push-ups or sit-ups that got me, it was the run. Nearly every run during the span of basic training- outside of the physical fitness test- we ran as a group, and I was one of the few that couldn't keep up. In the Army, if you can run you're a holy man, and if you can't you're some shameful abomination. The drill instructors placed the slowest people first to set the pace for the run, and I still fell behind every time. When you fall behind the entire group must circle back around, for you to fall back into rank, before proceeding. This happened more times than I can count.

Having flat feet and the inability to control my breathing was something I couldn't overcome. I was a great athlete in my youth, but distance running was not for me. The soldiers in my platoon hated me because I couldn't run. They questioned why a black guy who weighed a buck thirty-five, soaking wet, couldn't move his tiny body any faster. There were numerous occasions I was threatened with physical violence should I fall out of formation again. I can't blame them since I was routinely turning our three-mile runs into a five-mile runs. It seemed like I never improved, despite running every morning.

The final physical fitness test is pass or fail. A soldier must complete a certain number of push-ups, sit-ups and complete a two-mile run under a specific time, all scaled into age groups. If you failed any of these exercises, you had to start the nine-week training course all over again. As the end of basic training neared, I knew I was in trouble. Test day came around and I told myself that no matter what happened, I would fix my problem.

I felt like I started off quickly enough, but my peers continued to pass me. I could hear the drill sergeants calling out times for the guys finishing. I flew across the finish line wheezing, about to pass out and unsure of my time. Well, I scarcely passed by a mere six seconds. Six seconds away from having to go through basic training all over again. I was pumped about passing but pissed at the same time. I had to get better at running.

The problem remained with my unit in Arizona as I continued to fall out of our runs. The high elevation and thin air made Arizona a terrible place to run. it was a struggle to inhale enough oxygen. But I woke up one day and decided I was tired of letting people down and coming in dead last. I meditated on overcoming my addiction and all the struggles of my past, then focused my inner dialogue. I told myself, *"No more."* I wouldn't fall out again.

Every single morning, before 5:30 AM formation, I would get up and run two miles. I woke up and ran no matter what, on days we had conflicting plans, weekends, and days we already planned to run. I did that for two months straight. At first, no one noticed because it hadn't made a difference with the group, but in time, I became a running beast. I began running six-minute miles and finishing a two-mile run in under thirteen minutes. I ran an 11:30 two-mile on my next PT test; the fastest recorded time on-post at that moment.

People were shocked. The big question was how in the hell I had accomplished the improvement. It was simple. I was done sucking at running. I was done being last. It all came down to hard work to make the change in myself, rather than sit back and wish it would improve on its own. I wasn't afraid to lose sleep by putting in some extra effort, and in doing so, I became the best runner in my platoon. Once the fire is lit, there's no slowing me down.

A NEW LIFE

There are few happier moments in my life than the day I put my uniform on for the last time and said goodbye to the United States Army. The memory of it brings a smile to my face, the joy of being free. I paid my debt to this country, and it was time for me to move on. Now my attention was solely on putting together a successful civilian life.

At the time of my departure, I was in a four year relationship. In my experience with relationships, if it didn't end in marriage, it didn't end amicably. I did everything I could do to sabotage it. We had our season, as they say, but no matter how much we wanted it to work, we just weren't happy with the situation. I never wanted to join the statistic of being a single parent family, especially since my biological father did that to me. But I'm not my father and my heart has always been in the right place. Together, we had a handsome and intelligent son, my world, whom I love him and miss him with all my heart.

One must take note of the dependency a job like the military creates. Every two weeks, regardless of output, I consistently received a check for the exact same amount. Food was never scarce because even if I didn't buy groceries, I could go to the dining facility on-post and eat for practically free. If I needed a place to stay for a few nights, I could always stay in a barracks room until I found an alternative. The façade you build in your ability to manage your own life comes crashing down when enlistment is over. You find yourself with few skills applicable in the real world. The Army coddles you just enough to keep up retention, but once you're out you find yourself exposed and unprepared.

When my relationship ended, picking up the

pieces of my life had never been more difficult. I think the saying goes, *"it's cheaper to keep her"*. Since we had been living together, I had nowhere to go when we split. She kept the apartment, and our son, while I felt the burden of instability and homelessness. In times like that, I had limited friends to call upon for help due to my introverted personality. I eventually found an old military friend with the rectitude to let me crash on his couch for a few weeks. I stayed for a time, but concerns of not wanting to overstay my welcome crept into my mind. I didn't want to become a burden to a friend. With my thanks and no prospects for living arrangements, I went back out on the street.

I mismanaged my money poorly before that. I bought expensive things because I thought the stability of my relationship would last. We made a decent combined salary, but on my own I was a fish-out-of-water. I knew I wanted to get out of the relationship, but I didn't calculate the logistics of it actually ending. I lived paycheck to paycheck. It was more like surviving. Where was I going to go? How would I eat? How was I going to become successful? There had to be more to life. This couldn't be the outcome.

I started by managing a slow sales GNC, which was right up my alley because I live and breathe health, nutrition, and fitness. Even though I was the manager of the store and worked my butt off, my salary was peanuts. I received a commission but because the customer count was so low, I hardly made any extra money. I once worked an open to close shift and only two customers came the entire day. Managers from other stores often joked that my store cost the company more to keep open than actually profit from it and told me not to be surprised if I went in one day to find the lights shut off. I laughed alongside them but worried internally knowing there was some truth their jokes.

The first few nights on my own, I slept in my car, in middle of a cold Washington State winter, planning

my next moves. I had all the stuff that was important
to me tightly packed inside a solitary purple tote in the
back seat. Every night, before attempting to sleep, I
layered up in multiple sweatshirts and pants. I kept a
thick beanie on my head and wore a pair of old
military gloves. They were lifesavers. I didn't have a
pillow or blanket and no dispensary income to afford
them anytime soon. I tried my best to sleep but a
specific paranoia always set in when I tried to close my
eyes. It seemed, someone always seemed to park right
next to me even when I took refuge in secluded areas.
The whole parking lot could be completely empty, yet
someone always shot into the spot right next to me.
This and patrolling security vehicles creeping by
would always stir me from my sleep.

I worked all day, hopped in the car at night and
drove to the local Walmart about ten minutes away. I
read in a forum, after a Google search, that Walmart
was a safe place to sleep in your car. It was somewhere
the cops wouldn't hassle you as long as you kept a low

profile and stayed out of trouble. I get my restless sleep until morning, then go back to open the store. When I needed to shower I went to the local gym. Luckily someone always left soap in the showers because I couldn't even afford that much, and I didn't even have a towel so I used two t-shirts, one to wash and one to dry. I'd quickly clean up and prepare for another terrible night spent in my freezing car.

There were times I wished I could run my car's heater all night for warmth. How great it would have been, but I had little money and needed to conserve gas between paydays. My gas light was consistently on empty and I just couldn't risk wasting the last few drops.

One night I dozed off and was awoken by someone staring right at me with hands above his eyebrows peeking into my driver's side window. He was so close I could see the fog from his breath on the glass. I shot up in my seat, nerves racing. Startled, he took off running in the opposite direction. I gave thought to chasing him down, teaching him to mind his business, but did nothing since I was trying to keep a low profile.

I no longer felt safe so I took an alternative solution I had been debating to myself for a while. Being the manager of my store, I had a key that allowed me to come and go as I pleased. I also made the schedule for the employees, so I could easily make certain that I closed the store every night. That would allow me to discretely lock everything up, turn off the lights, and make my way to the backroom storage area for some shut-eye.

The store offered ample warmth but little for my peace of mind. Even inside the safety of the store, I was paranoid. I was breaking GNC policies and walking a fine line taking that chance. If someone had discovered me on the floor I could have easily been fired and, worse yet, potentially get law enforcement involved, but it was a risk I was willing to take.

Meanwhile, the funds in my bank account

continued to dwindle. I still had bills to pay and I still wanted to give financial support to my son. I tried to delay the issue but knew needed to share responsibility in providing for him. My ex-girlfriend was better off than me, she didn't need the money, but the morality of the situation made me look past my circumstances to pay what I could.

I regularly scrounged for change in crevices with the hopes of finding enough to get me by. My stomach growled ceaselessly, still accustomed to a full belly provided by the military. Once nighttime rolled around I'd go through the McDonald's drive-thru and order a couple bucks worth of food. Thank God for the dollar menu. That was my reward on particularly rough days. Two burgers and the occasional apple pie per night sustained me for a few months. Other times I'd have to make due with ramen noodles cooked in the store's microwave.

I was so desperate for money a few times that I would work ten-hour open to close shifts for the extra hours. Eventually, my regional sales director, RSD, told me I was only allowed forty hours a week and that I would be penalized for clocking anything over. Anything over forty hours required the company to pay time and a half, so they demanded employees not go into overtime or risk being fired. When the limited hours wouldn't cut it, I started dipping into the register at work.

Now hear me out, I have an ethical awareness, so I don't take pride in my actions. When you're in survival mode you take risks you'd normally avoid or never consider. I pocketed the cash register to pay bills and get by, sometimes that not a single dollar was left. I always scheduled the pull close to payday because I knew if I took money to pay bills, I could replace it within a couple days and shorten the chance of being discovered. Imagine my surprise when the RSD came in for a spontaneous theft check one morning. Half the money that was supposed to be in the cash register had been spent on bills.

It was pure luck the RSD took my word that the money was all accounted for. I like to think the universe finally paid me a solid that was long overdue. The bullet was dodged. After that close call I stopped. It was probably a safer bet to not pay my bills than ruin my work history or land in jail. Over time I was able to return every cent I took from the register.

I knew I couldn't stay there forever but life could have been worse off. I still trained at the gym during those times, that helped my mental fortitude. With headphones on and music blaring, a few hours at the gym helped the nights pass by faster. It also assured me I would be tired before laying my head down at night so I wouldn't have to think about my mess of a life.

Ever prideful, to a fault, I refused to be someone's burden because of the missteps I made. I never told my family about my situation. It was up to me to take responsibility for the outcome of my relationship and the financial dilemma I caused myself.

There was also the embarrassment to consider, although now I know what I went through is a common problem most would like to admit. The relationship was also beyond salvaging. It happened, I couldn't change it even if I wanted. There was no going back. What I needed was a fresh start. Instead of dwelling on the past, I had to start creating a future. I decided sleeping in my car was no longer viable. I had had enough of brutal winter nights spent curled up in the uncomfortable seats of my Chevy Impala.

I always knew that I wanted to return to North Carolina. I dated a girl in high school who I kept in touch with through every relationship. Even if it had been months, one of us always found a way to reach out to the other. I knew then, somehow, she was my soulmate. She was the one that got away. I had joined the Army when she became a freshman in college. As much as I wanted us to be together it just wasn't in the cards at that time in our lives, but I knew, wholeheartedly, that we would find our way back to each other.

I promised her that I would move back to North Carolina and give us another shot at some point. I told her that no matter where life took us, I would come back to marry her. It felt like a scene from a Nicholas Sparks movie where love always seems to win in the end. I'm sure she was skeptical, but she never showed it.

I told her that I was contemplating finally coming back home to the East Coast. I was done with everything the West Coast had to offer. I could no longer live with the thought of her finding someone else to settle down with. I set a specific date for my move. I didn't know exactly how it would happen, because I didn't have the money, but setting a date made it more concrete. I knew if I backed out after naming a specific date and getting her excited, I deserved to lose out on the potential of whatever we could be. I gave myself three months to get everything together and save as much as possible. An incident one night that would expedite my plans.

I was sleeping behind the cash register one night after a long day of work, something I did from time to time later on. It was out of sight from the storefront's window and was carpeted, whereas the rest of the floor was linoleum tile. I dozed off around thirty past midnight, content I was another day closer to moving, when I heard four loud thuds from the storefront. Something was hitting the glass.

You can imagine my panic. I automatically assumed that someone was breaking in through the front door. I was terrified, although in hindsight I bet my reaction looked hilarious. Years of military training kicked into gear as I low crawled fifteen feet from the cash register to the back room. I grabbed my keys and bolted out the back door, never once glancing back at the front to see what happening or if anyone was there. I just ran! I hopped in my car, peeled out of there, and headed to the Walmart where I regularly stayed.

I started parking my car in the back of the store a few weeks prior, in case the employees or regional managers made a late-night trip to the store so they couldn't see my bright red car sitting in the parking lot. I was scared out of my mind but debated whether or not I should call the police. How could I explain the store was in the process of being robbed while I was living there? I didn't know how I could explain the circumstances.

I waited a few hours for my nerves to settle. Once my shaking stopped, I drove past the store to check. Parts of the ten-foot glass storefront were cracked. I pulled my car up to the sidewalk and walked over to the glass to better inspect the four spider web breaks surrounding distinct holes. I looked down and saw about ten steel balls lying below the glass. They looked like BB gun pellets. Had the store become a casualty of a poorly executed, and clearly poorly funded, drive-by shooting? Someone apparently decided to riddle the front of my store with BBs.

I never called the cops because I wouldn't have been able to explain why I was at the store at that hour. That alone would make me a suspect, then I would have to explain the entire story. Back at Walmart, my mind raced. I returned to the store in the morning for my opening shift. I called the cops then. Afterward, I called my RSD and explained the situation. Strangely, nobody doubted the story I gave, which wasn't exactly the full truth. But I would have thought BBs shot at a store window might merit some questions, but no one did. Everything went smoothly.

A glass company came out to survey the damage and to board the space where the window had been. The wood covered the hole for a few days until the glass was replaced. I was well beyond sleeping in that store, and I never found out what really happened. It could have been teenagers fooling around, my ex-girlfriend asking someone to scare me, or maybe it

135

was an unhappy customer that didn't like a product I'd sold them.

I like to think it was the universe pushing me to do the thing I so desperately needed to do. It definitely got the ball rolling. Sleeping on the floor had become too risky. My whole lifestyle was dangerous. What if it had been actual rounds going through the window instead of BBs? I told Kimberly that I was coming back sooner than expected, and meticulously saved every dime I could for the next two weeks.

The weeks flew by and soon enough day of my departure arrived. I was nervous. I had a lot of anxiety about what I needed to accomplish. I set out on an adventure of a lifetime, in a car with little maintenance, two new tires (because I couldn't afford four), having done no research on which route I should take, and only $200 in my pocket. It was a trip that would intimidate most people, but for me, became something I'd come to see as an accomplishment.

THE TRIP ACROSS THE U.S.

I believe the universe speaks to people. It tends to open doors and present opportunities when it needs you to act. I also believe that anything worth doing is going to suck at the beginning until you break through to the other side. The universe doesn't make it easy to pass through these doors and gives only a short window of time to act on those opportunities. Your one shot can pass you by because you're too afraid of the risks involved. When the universe spoke that time, I ignored the risk and I acted.

I wanted to be in North Carolina, and only 3,000 miles of road stood in my way. On a beautiful spring day I typed *Raleigh, North Carolina*, into my GPS and hopped into my Impala. I had all my belongings inside a purple tote, a box of brown sugar Pop-Tarts and four NoDoz energy drinks. With no intentions of stopping, except to fill gas and take the occasional restroom break, I set off on the road. Sugary snacks would be my fuel for the next few days. My prepaid BlackBerry that had trouble picking up signal, even in populated areas, so it really served no purpose. I let my parents and my girlfriend know I was on the way. I was eager to see the woman I loved, Kimberly Turner. I couldn't linger around the West Coast anymore.

You might suppose that because I was prior military I would have made meticulous plans, like a mission of some sort. After all, my past is full of risk assessments and long drawn out briefings and debriefings. I could have considered the route, rest areas, restaurants, inclement weather and maybe even backup communication in case something were to happen. I should have planned my trip better, but I didn't. I've always been a spur of the moment kind of guy, and while I always enjoyed a drive, I underestimated just how grueling this coast to coast trek would be.

MY FIGHT WITH MONTANA

Montana. I am driving through mountainous areas, with no one in sight except the occasional tractor-trailer carrying loads across the country. I began to spot warning signs that all vehicles required snow chains on their tires before proceeding any further. I had never seen a sign like that before. Even if I had chains, which I didn't, I hadn't a clue how to put them on. The places I lived, where I was from, didn't require snow chains. With my back against the wall, I had to make a choice. I could reroute the GPS or continue forward with my original plan to push straight through. Stupid yes, but I wasn't about to find an alternate route and have the same thing happen on a different road.

I forgot about the signs an hour later, after I stopped seeing them posted on the side of the road. I wondered if maybe they were just cautions that applied to those traveling during snow season. I didn't even know when Montana's snow season started or ended, but sure enough, snowflakes began to fall. My elevation was increasing. The communities in the valleys below appeared small and distant. I never put two and two together. My cross-country trek would require me to clear actual mountains.

The snow started to pick up. Night came and there were hardly any street lights illuminating the road ahead of me. I checked my phone. No service. If there was an emergency, I'd be on my own. The few snowflakes multiplied and turned into a blizzard. I couldn't see anything in front of my car as snow built up on my windshield. I weighed the option to pull over and letting the storm pass. *"What if it doesn't stop snowing, I run out of gas, lose heat and then I freeze to death?"* I asked myself. No, not an option, I had to keep it moving.

It had been hours since I last saw another vehicle on the road. I was alone. No one knew where I was. If I got stuck the chance of someone finding me could be slim. I talked myself through it with positive thoughts. I told myself, *"It's only snow and people drive through snow storms all the time."* I even hyped up my car. *"You can do it Old Red, you've got over 100,000 miles on you already, why quit now? This is not how our story ends Old Red, we have too many more miles to cross."* I held on to any glimmer of hope that could keep me motivated to press onward.

I slowed my speed down to a crawl. It helped that every now and again a tractor-trailer would pass me out of nowhere and clear a little of the road for me to follow. I'm sure they were laughing at me out there and radioing one another about the little red car trying to brave the storm. But God bless those truckers. Those big rigs saved my life. A bit dramatic, maybe, but as the saying goes, you had to be there. I drove in the middle of the road, two hands on the wheel, with one thought in mind, "I am not dying here."

The nightmare eventually came to an end. The universe was done toying with me. The snow relented, and I could see the blacktop again. I was thrilled and relieved, but had to make up for the time I lost driving at a crawl. I stepped on the gas, accelerating up to 90 mph, confident I was leaving the worse part of my journey behind. I cranked the radio up, drank another NoDoz and tried to get out of Montana as quickly as possible.

I was cruising along when I noticed headlights flashing from behind me. They were regular headlights, and I assumed they wanted me to either pick up the pace or get out of the way. A part of my ego felt challenged. Did he think I was some pushover who would just move out of his way? Hell no! I stepped on the gas to well over 100 mph. The approaching car responded back with blue and red flashing lights, like the 4th of July.

There were lights everywhere, the top of the car, inside the windshield and even on the mirrors. The car I wanted to race was a Montana state trooper, the one trooper in the entire state. He had been tracking my car for almost twenty minutes. I aggressively braked and he pulled his car alongside mine, both of us at cruising speeds. He was scoping me out, trying to evaluate whether I was a threat or not. What he saw a middle-aged, bearded black man, with out of state plates and a black hoodie pulled over his head. On top of that, it was nighttime and I was doing speeds well exceeding the limit; textbook reckless driving. I was going to jail, I knew it. Out there, in the middle of nowhere, he could've easily shot me and dumped me on the mountain. No one would ever know. I usually don't agree with the rhetoric of a black man being shot for driving "while black", but I have to admit the experience puckered my ass.

I pulled over to the side of the road, placed two

hands on the steering wheel and asked the universe for the courage to get me through. In my side mirror, I could see a meager police officer, in his early twenties, step out of his vehicle and approach with a hand on his sidearm. He shone a light at the contents of my backseat. I waited, patiently, with the window down.

With a hostile tone, he asked me where I was coming from. I usually crack jokes when I'm anxious, but this was no time for humor, even nervous humor. I explained the situation, everything about my trip. I told him why I was there, all the way to up to having just come out of the blizzard. I took full responsibility for speeding and handed him everything he asked for, letting him know where I was reaching and what I was getting. I think my own tone deescalated the entire situation. He had every right to take me to jail that night. Instead, he dropped the ticket down to fifteen over the speed limit and let me go.

Keeping calm under pressure kept the situation from escalating into something ugly. The ticket was only forty dollars! I've received stricter fines for doing less. He even offered me the option to pay then and there, but I had to decline because of my limited funds. He thanked me for keeping a cool head, told me to drive safely, and even wished me luck that everything would turn out well. I went on my way, this time following the speed limit. I couldn't afford any more delays, I had places to go and people to see.

WHAT IS SLEEP?

After the setbacks with the snow and state trooper, I was well on my way. State welcome signs fed into my confidence. I was going to make it. The red colored road in Wyoming was one of the strangest things I'd seen. I crossed vast rolling hills, large expansive bridges, and saw goats on the sides of mountains. The weather was no longer an issue, and I was making amazing time. My biggest fear was getting stranded in the middle of nowhere, so I made certain there was enough gas in the tank. A flat tire would probably end my journey.

In all the madness, as exhausted as I was, it felt like I didn't need sleep. It was a forty-two-hour drive, and I was halfway through it without an ounce of shuteye. I kept going, kept driving, trekking towards my goal. Morning became night then night turned to day, all the while sustained on NoDoz and sugary Pop-Tarts. Sometimes I'd roll the window down and let the biting cold air wake me up, or crank the radio's volume to give me a musical jolt of energy. Singing along gave me something to do along spans of emptiness that would otherwise lull me to sleep. Of course my lack of sleep caught up to my body and mind.

Sleep deprivation washed over me. One minute I was yawning, the next my eyes completely glossed over. I couldn't see anything besides the blur of lights ahead of me. I tried to blink and shake my head rapidly to wake myself up, but nothing worked. It felt like I was completely drunk behind the wheel. I rubbed my eyes as hard as I could until things came into focus again. The effects lasted around twenty seconds but felt like a ten-minute battle. That was the end of my energy. I pulled into the next rest area the first chance I got.

The only vehicles parked were a few tractor-trailers. I set an alarm on my phone for an hour. I managed only fifteen minutes, anxiety keeping me awake. My thoughts raced, ready to hit the open road, ready to finish the trip. The odds of something going wrong increased with the more time I spent on the road. I also worried about falling to sleep in a dark secluded rest area. I've seen plenty of true-crime television shows. Last thing I wanted was to end up on an episode.

I stepped out into the frigid air and did 100 jumping jack then slapped myself in the face repeatedly, yelling at myself to finish for motivation. I was pumped, I was ready, I was wide awake. Other than two more five-minute naps at gas stations, I never went back to sleep. I was mentally drained but completely present as I sang each song on the radio and observed every road sign. My senses sharpened and I grew more aware with each state I crossed.

150

I made it to my parents' home in Virginia in just over two days, faster than what everyone anticipated. I smelled awful, my beard was nappy and the hair on my head was growing back in patches. I had so much plaque on my teeth they felt like velvet rugs. There was also a massive pimple on my face I hadn't noticed until I had the chance to relax and get a good look at myself.

I devoured everything in my parents' refrigerator because I hadn't eaten much in three days. I told them about my trip and they scolded me for not stopping and not preparing myself. I understood, but nothing could bring me down. Driving from one coast to the next, with limited money and resources is dumb, I realize that. I don't recommend it. But sometimes you do dumb scary things to make a change in your life. I was about to cultivate a successful life for myself. And first thing I had to do was find the one who got away.

THE CHANGING OF A SEASON

The move to North Carolina, turned out to be life-changing in many ways. Everything happened so fast. It was more than I could have imagined back when I roomed on the GNC floor and dreamt of flipping my life around. I was able to transfer my job at GNC to North Carolina. Although I was making the same pay, I started to build some financial stability. My bank account was out of the negative. At last, I could finally afford basic necessities.

I stayed with my aunt for a few months and established a new routine, much different from the one in Washington. Most of my free time was spent with Kim or at the gym, two things I never wanted to be away from. It felt like a huge weight lifted off my shoulders and finally felt optimistic about the future. For the first time in my life I could afford my own apartment. No more barracks room or car. I had my own place, a cozy little one-bedroom apartment with cheap amenities and outdated décor. Despite its shortcomings, I couldn't have cared less. For the first time in years, I was happy.

Kim and I decided to take things very slow and start our relationship off as friends. It had been years since we'd seen each other. We were, in a way, starting anew. We began by spending our days together. That turned into spending every night together and me inevitably asking her out. After dating a while she moved into my apartment. Kim was the exact same girl I had fallen in love with. Her smile, moral compass, and unmatched beauty never withered. She was still authentic through and through. We eventually married and had a beautiful little girl together. They are my entire world, and the very reason I work hard to make a great life for them.

When the time was right I took a shot at switching my career. I began to sour at the thought of working in retail. I despised sales and I couldn't bear being told what to do. I wouldn't sell products I didn't believe in. It was dishonest. My superiors hated that I only sold people what they needed, not what the company thought they needed. In the course of looking for opportunities elsewhere, I responded to an ad for personal trainers at a local gym. I had dabbled in personal training before and knew it could be a great opportunity to expand in a career I could enjoy. I got the job without a hitch, thanks to a great first impression- a useful skill to have.

I wanted to help people and I took pride in being the best personal trainer in the gym. The only problem was, the job came with a lot of pressure to sell, up-sell, and close the deal. It felt like I was selling cars rather than helping people reach their goal to become healthier versions of themselves. The owner of the gym had no reservations in pressuring people into training packages they couldn't afford. That was never my vision of how personal training should work. To them, a client was just another number, and when I realized this was the case I stopped enjoying my work. Nothing good would come from staying. As predictable as the seasons, change was on the horizon.

I had done my due diligence in learning how to structure a business, and how to get clients. I had put in the work and made a name for myself with honesty and providing amazing results. Right before I decided to put my knowledge to the test at a different gym, a local studio owner contacted me about an opportunity to work for myself. The universe was giving me a Hail Mary. I could make my own schedule, dictate pay, and be rewarded based on the effort I put in. I could choose who to work with and focus on getting the results each client needed with no pressure to sell. It was exactly the opportunity I needed.

I now own a health and fitness coaching company called TND Fitness- Tested Never Defeated.

It started with a simple but deep belief that no matter where we are in life, what we've been through, or what we will face, we're all tested but never defeated. Through hard work, embracing *the suck*, and extreme ownership of our mistakes, we can be better persons today than we were yesterday. It's a philosophy that applies to both mind and body.

My business has tripled over the last two years and it continues to grow. I've touched so many lives in such a short time, and now I can't imagine doing anything else with my life. I'm asked all the time what separates me from other trainers and I explain that I've crushed every single deterrent on my path, relying on pure resolute willpower, and unequivocally believe every person can learn to do the same. Now it's my job, my mission, to teach this control to others.

<u>LEARNING FROM MY</u>

<u>EXPERIENCES</u>

We are all going through our own trials-
addiction, illness, a job or relationship you can't stand
but don't have the courage to leave. Life is full of tests.
They can either destroy you or galvanize you into a
hardened badass. Sometimes we spend so much time
in the darkness it becomes our reality. I was there too,
miserable each and every day, pummeled by the
weight of the world. Whenever things were looking
brighter, I'd be swallowed back into the darkness.
Each time I made strides forward, a major setback
would push me back.

Giving into the first signs of despair strengthens
the darkness. I overcame my own difficult moments

because I pushed aside negative thought, and did something to improve the situation. With some luck, perseverance, and positive self-motivation, I dragged myself out. Yes, I was a reckless along the way, but sometimes you need to be in order to brave the storm. The cavalry was going to ride in and save me. I had to save myself. There was no use in complaining. If this was true, it meant there were only two other paths to take- lay down and quit or resist and make the future I wanted more than anything become a reality.

I wanted to give up. There were days when I wanted to end all the suffering. In my suffering I finally understood. I, like others out there, trapped myself in negativity and unrealistic expectations. The world owed me nothing, and seeing that hard, yet valuable truth, I changed my way of thinking. Rather than turn each hurdle into a hinderance they became motivational fuel, challenges waiting to become achievements. Each achievement, every struggle conquered, made me feel like a giant and the pain

158

from before seemed distant and brittle.

If you are going through an addiction trust the words of a man who's been down that route, you can get over it. Addiction happens to those who don't see their self-worth. Discover you worth. Love yourself. Change your thinking so that you're the most important person in the universe. Seek the help you need, whether through professional channels or someone you trust. There are countless stories of those who've conquered their addictions. There's no reason why your tale can't be among them. No, it's not something that will go away overnight. There's no one hour cure for the fight with addiction, but by fixing yourself and changing your ability to channel your pain into raw positive motivation you can leave addiction in the past as you enter a healthier future.

Every day someone receives a diagnosis that shakes them to their core. I know what it's like to be told your health is failing or that you have a disease you'll have to struggle with for the rest of you life. It's not easy news to digest, and when that bomb drops all you want to do is punch a hole in a wall or cry your eyes out- sometimes both. It's okay to feel those emotions, but it's dangerous to harbor them. If you can't let those feelings come and go they'll start to poison the way you think.

The world is waiting for you to set an example, and the one you choose is how people will treat you. If you play the victim people will grow accustomed to treating you as such. They might even pick up and share the habit by adopting their own victim-centric mentality. Or you can take a stand and show others the fight you have inside, and in doing so become a source of inspiration for them. Someone is always observing our actions and behavior, how we manage stress, whether it's a spouse, a friend, or more importantly children. I strive to maintain control and composure when times get painful so they can learn from my own discipline in the example I set.

Most importantly, be kind. Everyone is fighting a

battle you know nothing about. How you treat someone can make or break how they proceed in coping with their own tribulations. Being charitable to others releases a rush of endorphins. Your body is designed to reward your kindness with happiness. Give back to the world with a smile and the universe will reciprocate..Maybe not immediately but always inevitably. Start small, with obtainable goals. Say something motivational to at least one person every day. Hold yourself accountable for doing them, write it down if you must. Track the days you fail and the days you succeed. After a few weeks it becomes a habit, and you're well on your way to developing positive momentum.

Once the momentum of you deeds starts to really propel you life in a better direction. You'll look back and hardly recognize the person you were before, the one wallowing in a cloud of doubt and self-loathing.

Life will test you every single day, every step of

the way. Don't run from pain, take your lumps and grow. It's a part of life, a part of being alive. I hope my story, what I've given you in this book, is some fuel for your fight. Take the wisdom of a man who's been down a few of rough roads of his own. Embrace the suck. Embrace the pain. It all makes wonderful material for building your character.

It's a philosophy no different than lifting at the gym. Every weight is a challenge, a heavy burden opposing your strength. It's up to you to go in each day to train, build a resistance, overcome new hurdles, and defy the odds. Like gravity, events in life are going to naturally push you down. It happens to the best and worse of us. All we can do is push back, one set, two sets, three sets, until you've become someone else entirely, someone stronger and healthier. *"Tested, never defeated"*. It's my motto, my mantra.

I BELIEVE IN YOU

I want to leave you with four words, four words that can spark action but are said far too infrequently, despite the strength they carry. I BELIEVE IN YOU! Yes, I BELIEVE IN YOU! No, I'm not just blowing steam. No, I'm not trying to invoke some emotion that ultimately leaves you with a false sense about what you can achieve. I have no ulterior motives here. I adamantly and sincerely believe in you.

I believe in what you can become. You're stronger than your doubts. You were put here with a purpose and the ability to achieve that purpose, but I think you fear the responsibility of action or fear what you can become- POWERFUL BEYOND MEASURE.

I've survived my battle with Crohn's and kidney disease, addiction, and living with no roof over my head. From a depression that nearly claimed my life, to this rebirth as a motivator, bodybuilder, fitness guru, and life coach, realize you can do it too. It is achievable. Whatever fight you are in, whatever cloud hangs over your head, I believe you can weather the storm and find your destiny. Hold true to your faith that you will endure. You will make it to the other side.

Can you see it? A life with purpose, filled with dreams and manifested aspirations? Can you see your reflections as you grow into an unstoppable human being, like a phoenix rising up from the ashes of their past to burn brighter than ever before. Can you see your brilliant leading others, casting out their own shadows and doubts? Can you see what I see in you?

I believe. Do you?

About the Author

Bryant Reed is a United State Army veteran with twenty-seven months spent in combat zones as an interrogator. He is currently the owner of Tested Never Defeated Coaching in North Carolina. There, he's able to reshape lives and bodies with his philosophy of positivity. Maintaining a clientele of over twenty-five individuals, Bryant Reed spends his days inspiring others to lead fit and healthy lives, physically and mentally. In 2016 he competed in North Carolina's *Golds Classic,* a bodybuilding competition, and won first place. He's also competed in several marathons, including Spartan runs, and spends time sharing his story as a motivational speaker. *Tested Never Defeated* is his debut book.